THE PROFESSOR AND THE PROSTITUTE

And Other True Tales of Murder and Madness

Linda Wolfe

BALLANTINE BOOKS • NEW YORK

Some of the pieces in this book first appeared in abbreviated form in *New York Magazine*.

Library of Congress Catalog Card Number: 86-397

ISBN 0-345-34367-0

First published by Houghton Mifflin Company. Reprinted by permission of Houghton Mifflin Company.

Manufactured in the United States of America

First Ballantine Books Edition: August 1987

For
M.P. and J.P.W.

Crime has been greatly on the increase among the lower classes [but] what strikes me as the strangest thing is that in the higher classes, too, crime is increasing proportionately. In one place one hears of a student's robbing the mail on the high road; in another place people of good social position forge false banknotes; in Moscow of late a whole gang has been captured who used to forge lottery tickets, and one of the ringleaders was a lecturer in universal history; then our secretary was murdered from some obscure motive of gain.... How are we to explain this demoralization of the civilized part of our society?

—Fyodor Dostoyevsky,
Crime and Punishment

Contents

Introduction

The stories collected here are not about murder and madness—mania, paranoia, sociopathy—among people who inhabit the middle class. My protagonists are doctors, academics, businessmen, schoolteachers, people who inhabit the middle class. My protagonists are doctors, academics, businessmen, schoolteachers, and the children of such individuals, the kinds of people I, and many others like me, might know, entertain, work beside.

As a reader, I've always been most drawn to books about people with whom I could identify. When it comes to true crime stories, books about upper-crust villains who knock off their heiress wives or their miserly fathers in order to collect more millions, or about lower-depth, deprived poor devils who kill at the drop of a wallet or go crazy from the sheer shambles of their surroundings never entirely appeal to me. The lives of the leading figures seem remote. I like meeting on paper individuals I recognize, wandering in a world that is, somehow, familiar. And if ever I feel I'm being parochial in my taste, I remind myself that the novel came about in the eighteenth century because suddenly there was a new class of people—the middle class—and they wanted to read works about themselves or people like them.

All of this is by way of explaining why it was that when, in the mid-1970s, I first began to write about murderers and maniacs, sociopaths and suicides, I always chose to explore the lives of individuals from my own background. But there was something more. It seemed to me that one of the most important questions a writer might address when writing of crime and craziness was: "Am I capable of committing a crime or of suddenly going haywire?" It is a question that haunts many people when they hear of someone they've known who has gotten into trouble with the law or unexpectedly killed himself, and it always used to tantalize me. I wanted to address that question, but I felt that the motivations and even the psychology of the very rich and the very poor were so different from my own that I couldn't really put myself in their place. So, remembering the age-old admonition to writers, "Write about what you know," I stuck to criminals and disturbed characters who inhabited, as I did, the great middle of society.

Although I'm a "psychological" writer, concerned with what lies beneath the surface of behavior, I see my decision to write about murder and madness as primarily a literary matter. In the late 1950s, I was studying for a graduate degree in literature, teaching English at a college, and writing short stories. I had little use for journalism then. Fiction, I felt, was the only suitable practice for a writer seeking to maneuver the minds of men and women.

I'd learned this from my professors, who almost never discussed nonfiction except for works of criticism and literary biography. I suppose I was provincial, but I was a product of my times. Tom Wolfe (no relation of mine, I'm sad to say) has written of literary values in the fifties: "The literary upper class were the novelists. They were regarded as the only 'creative' writers, the only literary artists. They had exclusive entry to the soul of man, the profound emotions, the eternal mysteries." As to journalists, "They were regarded chiefly as day laborers who dug up slags of raw information for writers of higher 'sensibility' to make better use of." Not wanting to be a mere documentarian—for that's how I viewed journalists—I concentrated on writing fiction.

By the early 1960s, however, having realized I was a writer and not a scholar, I'd given up teaching and graduate school and taken a job at Time Inc. I was in the belly of the journalistic whale, but I ignored my surroundings. A researcher by day, at night I went home and worked on short stories. But something was happening to me. I felt frustrated by the work I was producing. I wanted to tell *stories*, to have an engine on my tales that would drive them from suspenseful opening scenes to ironic or moving ends. But for the most part I was dwelling on my own psyche and limited experience of life, and my work seemed to lack narrative drive. I yearned to sprinkle the salt of plot over my paragraphs, but plots didn't come to me. My imagination was, I decided, impoverished.

Around that time, I began to collect newspaper articles that might trigger my recalcitrant imagination. I have them still, in a graying folder full of yellow clips: June 8, 1962, "Still No Clue to Killer. Five days of questioning have given Topeka police a fair outline of Daphne Rhodes' habits, an incomplete outline of her last hours alive, and no single useful clue to her killer. Since the 26-year-old New York divorcée was found raped and strangled in her apartment Sunday,

a two-man team of detectives has repeatedly questioned the small circle of Menninger Clinic patients
who were her friends and rechecked her apartment
in a fruitless hunt for leads." August 21, 1967, "Body
of American Missing in Prague Is Found in River. A
body identified as that of Charles H. Jordan, an American official of a Jewish relief organization, was found
today in the Vitava River in Prague. An examining
physician in Prague said the body had been in the
water for several days. He was unable immediately to
give the cause of death."

I felt a little embarrassed by that folder of mysterious tragedies and hid it in the back of a drawer. But I
knew by then (not that I'd learned it in college or
graduate school; those were the days of the so-called
New Criticism, and we studied almost exclusively an
author's output, not his sources) that many of the
writers I admired had treated themselves to the inspi-
ration of current events. Defoe had read accounts
about a man marooned on a desert island, and created
Robinson Crusoe. Flaubert had been told by a friend
about a doctor's dissatisfied wife who'd killed herself
after having a series of lovers, and invented *Madame
Bovary*. Dreiser had collected news stories about an
ambitious shirt factory foreman who had drowned his
pregnant millhand girlfriend in order to marry a so-
cialite, and brought forth *An American Tragedy*. I
kept hoping that the news events I was clipping
would help me write richer fiction.

Also, around that time, the late 1960s, a new kind
of journalistic work began to appear. In 1965, Tru-
man Capote's *In Cold Blood* was published. He called
it a "nonfiction novel," a term that irritated a lot of my
academic friends, but the book did indeed have many
of the elements of a novel—a strong sense of place,

characters whose internal thoughts as well as external acts were explored, and, most important, sequential action. In 1969, Norman Mailer published *Of a Fire on the Moon*, in which he himself became a character in the marvel of the moon shot. Gay Talese was writing about *Times*men as if he had access to the pathways of their neural space. Tom Wolfe was turning English on its head and making *me* dizzy, euphoric. Journalism had become more personal and unpredictable, and consequently suddenly exciting to me.

It was then that the idea first occurred to me that instead of using real events to fuel my fiction, I might try using fictional techniques to fuel nonfiction. I looked at my mystery clips and thought how challenging it would be to find out more about the events they described and, employing dialogue, dramatic scenes, and sequential action, try to turn some of them into nonfiction short stories. If I did, I thought, I'd never reproduce verbatim, as some nonfiction writers were doing (and regrettably still do), the bleak bones of research such as court transcripts, police records, and meandering interviews, but I'd rely on the selectivity that the pursuit of fiction had taught me, the discipline of making each detail telling and pace more prominent than packing.

I didn't, however, get the opportunity to try out my idea until the mid-1970s. Then I had what I will always think of as, callous though it may seem, the good fortune to have known someone involved in the kind of enigmatic tragedy I had habitually been clipping and was longing to write about: Cyril and Stewart Marcus, twin gynecologists, had been found dead from mysterious causes in a littered, garbage-ridden New York apartment; I had once been a patient of

Stewart Marcus. I was able to convince *New York* magazine to let me write about the brothers.

I later wrote a novel, *Private Practices*, that was inspired by the situation of the twins. But I had been bitten by the bug of actuality. And soon I began to concentrate on writing nonfiction accounts of murder and madness that tried at once to give the facts but also to let the story *unfold*, to emulate the short story by offering scenes and creating a feeling of immediacy.

I wrote the pieces that appear in this volume between 1975 and 1985. "The Professor and the Prostitute," which comes first, was the last one I did, and it comes closest to what I had in mind when I first dreamed about making real events read like invented tales. Here, more than in any of the other, shorter pieces, the information gathered from interviews, transcripts, police records, and the like is buried in a snug narrative nest. But all the strands of that nest, even the lines of dialogue and paragraphs of interior musings, come from court documents or interviews.

Curiously, however, having at last taken a stylistic idea and gone with it as far as I could, I began to feel its confines. One is limited by available facts. The mind cries out to know the things one wasn't told, could not discover. What did the professor's wife *really* think about her disloyal husband? What did the prostitute's parents *really* think about their risk-taking daughter? There are things nonfiction accounts can never tell us, for invariably some of the principals of a story will not cooperate, or they hide their true feelings, or they are simply not in the habit of probing their minds and motivations to the extent, or with the depth, that a writer requires. Thus to attempt to dramatize real events while forcing oneself to stick to available source material is to be in a new kind of writerly prison, the victim not of impoverished imagination but of inventiveness longing to swirl free.

Well, that's a writer for you—never satisfied. As Philip Roth has written, "If you want to be reminded of your limitations virtually every minute, there's no better occupation to choose. Your memory, your diction, your intelligence, your sympathies, your observations, your sensations—never enough."

One last word. I mentioned that I wanted to explore, in my pieces, the question of whether I myself could do the things my characters did. Whether the reader could. Today, these questions seem almost quaint to me, but at the time I began to write about murder and madness, I was under the sway of that pop psychology tenet that holds that the murderer, the swindler, the matricide and patricide, even the infanticide, are people "just like us." We all harbor aggressive thoughts, feelings of entitlement, surges of wrath and rage, goes that argument. And thus we too might one day, under certain stresses, experience fates like those of some of the people described in this book.

My investigations taught me otherwise. Often, when I'd begin researching a story about some startling act committed by an apparently upstanding middle-class citizen, an act of self- or other-directed destruction, it would appear that the aberrant deed that had captured my interest had happened out of the blue. But delving invariably revealed that my protagonists had a history of psychological instability. They acted, not out of the blue, but out of markedly gray troubled pasts. They suffered from psychiatric diseases like mania, severe depression, or drug abuse, or classic emotional character disorders, like sociopathy or hysteria.

No doubt there is, somewhere, a fine humanitarian impulse behind our willingness to believe that those who are violent toward themselves or others are people just like us. But to some extent we hold this belief out of ignorance of how certain personality disorders and psychiatric illnesses can foreshadow chaos and catastrophe. The stories in this book shed light on this matter and attempt to convey all I have learned, in the course of writing them, about the psychological forces behind tragic and mystifying events.

THE PROFESSOR AND THE PROSTITUTE

Boston, Massachusetts

1983

From the moment I first heard about the case of William Douglas, a professor at a medical school in Boston accused of murdering a young prostitute with whom he had fallen in love, I was intrigued. Naturally, I wondered if the professor had killed the prostitute. But more than that, I wondered about the love affair. I found the notion of a respectable man losing his heart to a hooker fascinating.

I wouldn't be the first writer to do so. The love of a professor for a prostitute had inspired Heinrich Mann's Professor Unrat (made famous by the Von Sternberg film The Blue Angel). *Dostoyevsky had written about a scholar's passion for a prostitute in* Notes from the Underground, *then returned to the subject two years later, creating a similar entanglement for Raskolnikov in* Crime and Punishment. *Anatole France, Somerset Maugham, Émile Zola, and a host of other writers had also addressed the matter, probing in powerful novels and short stories the love of reputable males for reprobate females. Something about such relationships tantalizes the imagination.*

No doubt this is because they speak to a secret part of ourselves, a place where reason disappears and fantasy takes over. To love a prostitute, to enter her world of unbridled sexuality, is an archetypal fantasy for men, just as to be a prostitute, to be free of the inhibitions of society, is an archetypal one for women.

In April 1983, I determined to write about Douglas and went to New England to research the story and attend the trial. Shortly after I started, Douglas, who had been maintaining his innocence for over a year, unexpectedly confessed to having killed his prostitute-sweetheart, Robin Benedict. The murder mystery was solved. But I continued my exploration, for to me there had all along been something far more compelling about the story than knowing whether or not the professor had killed the prostitute. It was the drama of fantasy made real.

The Professor in Nighttown

One night in March 1982, William Henry James Douglas, a professor of anatomy and cellular biology at Tufts University's School of Medicine in Boston, decided, as he often did when he worked late into the night, that he was too keyed up to go directly home and to bed. His work was intricate, demanding. He needed to relax; he needed a drink. Sex. A way of losing the self by embracing another.

A different man might have gone home, poured himself a Scotch, and, placing a needy, affectionate hand on his wife's sleeping body, awakened her to his troubles and his longing. But for Douglas, such an act was out of the question. He and Nancy, married for two decades and the parents of three children, hadn't made love in years. Indeed, he felt he no longer loved her, at least not in the romantic way he yearned to be in love. And when, recently, Nancy had taken a night job in a nursing home, he hadn't tried to discourage her, hadn't even raised the slightest objection. What difference did it make when they no longer even slept in the same room?

Forty years old and feeling that life had passed him by, Douglas packed up his briefcase, shut the door to his malodorous laboratory, and hurried through the empty, echoing corridors of the medical school. He

5

would go to a bar, he decided. Maybe even get himself a prostitute. It wouldn't be the first time. And where was the harm, as long as Nancy and the children didn't know?

A few moments later, he was strolling down the streets of Boston's red-light district, known as the Combat Zone, an area of strip joints, peep shows, and pornographic bookshops, or garish, multicolored light bulbs and crude signs advertising such attractions as "Live Acts Live!" and "Nude College Girls!"

The Zone is a small area, a mere four blocks or so. And it is so close to Boston's new cultural center and to several of the city's most prominent hotels that ordinary citizens frequently wend their way through. But its natural denizens are pushers, pimps, and prostitutes, and they are so frenzied that even the police who patrol the area speak of them with a certain amount of astonishment. "Sometimes I don't believe the kinds of characters we've got here," one member of the squad that polices the mean streets said to me. "I wish I could show you the footage we shot of activities in the Zone, things like the frames where one girl, pissed off at a customer, stands in the parking lot arguing with him and then suddenly grinds out her cigarette in his cheek." He went on to mention that muggings and knifings, beatings and thefts, were commonplace, and that even killings were not entirely rare.

Bill Douglas wasn't fearful. Perhaps he felt his bulk protected him. He was tall and weighed close to 275 pounds. Or perhaps he felt at ease because he knew the Zone well. It abuts the soaring, sterile architecture of the medical school, and ever since he'd jointed Tufts a few years before, he'd made frequent forays into the area. Whatever the reason, he shuffled slowly down one of the Zone's side streets, peering into the most popular hangouts, and finally slipped into a bar called Good Time Charlie's.

When I visited Charlie's, I was struck by the fact that despite its cheerful, backslapping name, it was extremely dreary. The customers, chiefly young sailors or seedy, down-at-the-heels foreigners, looked more lonesome than libidinous. Downcast, they drooped forlornly over their drinks, sipping steadily and eyeing with a minimum of interest the topless and bottomless dancers bumping and grinding mechanically to the sounds of a distant jukebox. Even when a tune ended and the dancers, in whatever state of undress they found themselves, climbed down from the overhead runway and perambulated through the smoky bar to put fifty cents in the jukebox, they—and the nearness of their naked flesh—did not seem to arouse the lethargic, lonely drunks.

Of course, the dancers weren't much to look at. They were, for the most part, bony or flabby or haggard. Nor were most of the prostitutes who frequented the bar particularly appealing. They were getting on in years; their expressions were obscured beneath heavy coats of makeup; their clothes were garish. But oddly, here and there, were some young prostitutes who were fresh-faced, beautifully built, handsomely dressed.

I'd come to Charlie's with a friend, a prosperous, proper Bostonian who'd never been in a Zone bar before but had agreed to accompany me for my safety's sake and also, I suppose, out of curiosity. All evening, as I interviewed the bartender and several prostitutes who had known Robin Benedict, my friend kept saying, "How could a man like Douglas—an academic

—be attracted to women like these? Sex, yes. But attracted? *Involved*?" He was disdainful, uncomprehending. Yet, before the night was out, he would alter his views. One of the handful of beautiful, well-groomed prostitutes approached him, and soon he was buying her drinks and listening to the story of her life.

She was young, dressed in an Ultrasuede suit, wore her hair in a librarian's twist, and spoke impeccable Boston English. Once, when she got up for a moment, my friend whispered to me, "I'm getting a bit of insight into your professor now."

The woman who'd picked up my friend was called, she told him, Sabrina, and when he asked her what a nice girl like her was doing in a place like Charlie's, she said—and he liked believing her—that she was here just temporarily. As soon as she got a bit of a nest egg together, she'd be going back to her studies, finishing her M.A. in anthropology at Boston University. My friend was fascinated and talked with her animatedly, only to be bitterly disappointed when the manager of Good Time Charlie's suddenly arrived, and, worried that we might be detectives, shooed Sabrina out of the bar.

Robin Benedict must have been a lot like Sabrina. Certainly, she was beautiful, slim and willowy with wide dark eyes, luxuriant raven-colored hair, and smooth pale skin with an underglow of topaz and tourmaline. She dressed conservatively, wearing slacks or skirts with matching blazers. And she had a lively, outgoing manner, a high-spirited way of putting shy men at east.

Douglas, a diffident man and always something of an observer from the sidelines, may have noticed these appealing traits about Robin and, attracted by them, put down his drink and tried to strike up a conversation with her. Or she may have addressed him first, sliding onto a barstool alongside him and offering him the usual Good Time Charlie's invitation to sex, "Hey, honey, lookin' to go out tonight?"

What is certain is that within minutes of their first conversation, Robin Benedict took William Douglas to a trick pad she had rented on Boston's fashionable Beacon Street.

I'd always thought of Beacon Street as the home of Boston's most affluent Brahmins, and certainly it retains that reputation in the national consciousness. But while the old, elegant town houses still line the street, most are no longer occupied by individual families. They have been converted into compact condominiums, headquarters for college associations, or small, shabbily decorated furnished apartments. Students and young, poorly paid professionals rent the apartments, but so too—often without the other occupants' realizing it—do prostitutes. Apparently they have many johns with a sexual preference for erotic activity at a good address.

William Douglas had sex on Beacon Street with Robin Benedict that night, staying with her for half an hour and paying her the obligatory $50. Then he went home to the suburbs.

Perhaps, when he got there, he looked in on his sleeping children, fifteen-year-old Billy, fourteen-year-old Pammy, and twelve-year-old Johnny, and afterward had his favorite late-night snack, milk and cookies. Or perhaps he went into his bedroom, delved into the recesses of his closet, and got out his pornography collection, books and magazines with titles like *Gang Up on Gail*, *Little Sarah's Slave Training*,

Forced to Submit, and *Illustrated Gang War Torture*, stacks of ads recommending massage parlors and escort services, and folders of newspaper articles about prostitutes.

Robin returned to Good Time Charlie's. Possibly when she did she stopped for a minute to talk with the only close girlfriend she had there, another prostitute named Savitri Bisram. Perhaps Robin and Savi relaxed for a few moments, giggling about the fat man's funny speech and his unfortunate looks. Douglas had a hesitant way of expressing himself, a recessed chin, thin lips, and, for all his girth, tiny hands and feet. But more probably Robin simply sauntered into Good Time Charlie's, surveyed the men at the bar, and found herself another john. Robin sometimes made as much as $1,200 a night. "Her typical workday," Douglas would later say, his words betraying a certain amount of grudging admiration, "was from three-thirty or four o'clock in the afternoon until at least three and usually until four in the morning."

The home to which Douglas returned that night was in Sharon, Massachusetts, a neat, relatively new suburb, popular with liberal, community-minded young families. Douglas's house was on Sandy Ridge Circle, a well-landscaped street a few minutes' drive from the center of town. Here the houses, many with bay windows, fireplaces, and broad porches, have basketball nets in the driveways and bicycles, tricycles, and automotive toys scattered on the lawns. Sharon, and in particular Sandy Ridge Circle, is a fine place to bring up children.

Bill and Nancy had moved there as soon as he'd received his appointment at Tufts in 1978. It was only about a thirty-minute drive to the medical school, and it had a good school system. Bill Douglas worried about things like that. He placed great store in education.

He'd come by his the hard way. The child of lower-class parents—his mother, an immigrant from Germany, had been a maid, his father a plumber—he'd had to work during his high school days in upstate New York and to attend a less than distinguished government-subsidized teachers' college, Plattsburgh State, in Plattsburgh, New York. While he was in college, his father died in a construction accident. There was no money for graduate school. Bill finished Plattsburgh, married Nancy, a heavyset, plain young woman, and settled down to life as a small-town high school science teacher. He had gone as far academically as he could afford to go. But after a year or two of teaching, he applied for and managed to obtain a National Science Foundation fellowship for a year of postgraduate study at Yale.

The intellectual atmosphere of New Haven altered Douglas, made him more ambitious. He began to dream of becoming a researcher and a professor, not just a science teacher, and when his year at Yale was up, he sought other grants and continued his postgraduate studies at Brown University. His mother was dead by then, but he had a new family. Nancy had given birth to Billy and Pammy. In 1970, a young father who had made his way to broad intellectual horizons despite inauspicious beginnings, he received his Ph.D. and landed his first college position, as associate professor of biology at Edinboro State College in Pennsylvania.

Bill did well at Edinboro, garnering praise from students and supervisors alike. But the school was a backwater and he longed now to be in the scientific swim. A year after starting at Edinboro, he found himself a new position, a research job at a private institution, the W. Alton Jones Cell Science Center in Lake Placid, New York. There he would be director of the center's electromicroscopy facility as well as associate director of education.

Once in Lake Placid, he quickly began making a name for himself in research circles. His field was tissue culture, and he specialized in studies that involved isolating cells and then growing them outside the body—a process known as in vitro, or in test tube, research. He worked on many projects, among the most elegant of which were his studies of surfactant, a waxy substance secreted in the lungs that permits them to inflate and deflate properly, but that is absent in the lung tissue of infants born prematurely.

He also applied himself to family life. Nancy, no doubt affected by the currents of the women's movement that were sweeping the country in the early seventies, had decided to go back to school to study nursing. She had also given birth to their third child, John. Bill tried to be a modern father, assisting with household chores and taking an active role in his children's lives. He chaperoned them on camping trips, chauffeured them to speed-skating lessons, and became the local peewee hockey coach. He also tried to be loving toward Nancy, once taking an entire week off from his job in order to nurse her after she'd had a miscarriage.

But most of the time what he did was work. His industry was prodigious. He began publishing regularly in scientific journals and soon was serving on their editorial boards. He began submitting remarkably well received grant applications to private foundations and the National Institutes of Health and soon was serving on the NIH's review panels, overseeing and evaluating the work of his peers. He took on additional responsibilities by teaching at his alma mater in Plattsburgh and at nearby North Country Community College as well. And he became a consultant for the American Cancer Society and for the Department of Medicine at Memorial Hospital in Pawtucket, Rhode Island.

Then, in 1978, he at last entered the scientific big time. Tufts University made him an offer, and he left Lake Placid to become an associate professor at the Tufts Medical School. He was still extremely industrious, and he taught, as well, in the university's dental and veterinary schools. Wherever he taught, he was much appreciated by students. At the medical school, he was consistently voted the best teacher in his department. One student told me that he was enormously considerate, always willing to answer questions or go over material that was complex; another said that of all his teachers, Douglas was the most concise and easy to understand.

But, like most academic scientists, Douglas's heart was in his research, and it was to this that he primarily devoted himself. In the next handful of years, he published more than sixty articles in prestigious scientific journals and applied for and received so many research grants that his lab became the busiest and most richly endowed in the Department of Cellular Biology and Anatomy.

There, he was engaged in myriad projects. A famous one, sponsored by the New England Anti-Vivisection Society, involved developing an alternative to the Draize technique, a method of testing the toxicity of cosmetics intended for human use by inject-

ing their chemical components into the eyes of rab-
bits. But he was doing research for the U.S. Navy as
well, and continuing his efforts to culture surfactant
outside the body, and traveling to scientific confer-
ences all over the country and in Europe. As one of
his colleagues said, "His achievements were not obscure and unimportant. They were serious and co-
gent projects which made notable contributions to
science." Bill Douglas was, in 1982, on his way to
becoming a major American scientist.

After his first meeting with the vivacious young prostitute, the distinguished professor got in touch with
her again and saw her three times in the next two
weeks. Each time, she gave him half an hour. Each
time, he gave her $50. They met late at night and
spent the expensive half hour in Robin's Beacon
Street apartment. It was sparsely furnished. She kept
in it only the barest essentials—a bed, a nighttable, a
dresser—and a handful of clothes, all of them robes.
She didn't really live in the apartment, she explained
to Bill. Her home, her real home, was in Natick, some
twenty miles away. She didn't tell him she lived there
with the man who had introduced her to prostitution.

Could he see where she lived? he asked her once.
He was intrigued by her.

She promised to take him there someday. And she
suggested that in the future the two of them spend an
hour together. Bill agreed. He was to say later, "My
feelings at that time were that she was very nice to
me, and enjoyable to be with."

Those first weeks of their relationship were astonishing to him. He had disported himself with prostitutes
before, always careful to conceal the practice from

Nancy by telling her that he had to stay late in his lab or return to it after dinner because he was under great pressure. This was easy, since he genuinely felt tense and pressured most of the time and, both at Lake Placid and at Tufts, he had gotten into the habit of working in his lab until well after midnight. It was only later that, secure in the knowledge that both his family and his colleagues were asleep, he would seek sexual surcease. But while he had known prostitutes, he had never known one like Robin. She was not only sexually inventive, but so glamorous that she stirred in him more than physical passion. She aroused in him fantasies about love that had haunted him since his adolescence. He found himself wishing he could just hold her hand and go walking with her on the Boston Common, take her sunbathing on some secluded beach, find an idyllic river and spend an afternoon canoeing. He wanted to share cultural experiences with her, too, and romantic, candlelit dinners.

One day he confessed these yearnings to Robin, who offered to make his dreams come true. And soon, just as he'd fantasized, they began to go to the movies together, to attend concerts and plays, to take drives in the country, and to stroll on the Common, feeding the ducks with little bits of bread. But Robin was a businesswoman, and she exacted her price. She demanded that Bill pay her $100 an hour for whatever they did together, whether it was having oral sex or buying pizza by the slice and eating it on a park bench, whether it was having anal sex or sitting cross-legged on the grass, sharing soulful reminiscences. One night, remembering his wish, she took him to her apartment in Natick and cooked dinner for him. She charged him not just for the ingredients and the time she spent shopping for and preparing the food, but also for the time she spent eating it with him. The evening cost him several hundred dollars.

Bill didn't care. He not only felt like a boy again but in some way was a boy again. At his desk in the lab, he scrawled long letters to her, pouring out his adoration in gushing, adolescent sentiments and a large, open handwriting. "Dearest Robin," he wrote her, his sentences tumbling to the very edges of the note-paper, "Knowing you has made my life brighter and happier. You are a remarkable, wonderful woman and being with you makes me a very fortunate man." "Dear," he wrote her, "You are a beautiful person and deserve only the very best in life!"

One night at midnight, he took her to see the movie to which all the young couples of the time were flocking, *The Rocky Horror Picture Show.* Then, just as all the young couples were doing, they went to see it again. Then again. And again. *The Rocky Horror Picture Show* cost him $800.

By May of 1982, he couldn't get enough of her. She flattered him. She called him her "favorite prof." She expressed interest in his research. And he began to see her as someone she wasn't, as a girl with rare artistic and musical abilities and a mind that was just crying out for knowledge. He wanted to meet her friends and family and to educate her, to play Pygmalion to her Galatea. In a way, his way, he was in love.

What kind of man falls in love with a prostitute to-day, when sexual companionship is relatively easy to come by? The answer is, of course, a repressed man, a lonely, insecure man. Other men, reaching the height of their careers and experiencing classic midlife yearnings, tend to solve their longing for a new and vital romantic attachment differently, particularly if, like Douglas, they have power and favors to dispense. They have affairs with interesting colleagues or ambitious young protégées. They divorce and remarry. That Douglas's solution was different has much to do with the fact that, for all his professional success, he was socially inept, an outsider.

He never had many friends. People who knew him during his years in Lake Placid told a reporter he would become silly after having a drink or two and that it was difficult to have a conversation with him. They thought he had a drinking problem or that he considered friendship frivolous. At Tufts it was the same. "He was very shy," said one fellow scientist. "He was very reserved," said the acting chairman of his department. "The only topic he ever felt comfortable discussing was the lab," said Professor Ronald Sanders, a colleague who had known him for years. "He simply never spoke about anything but our work. And that was true whether we were here in the lab or had gotten together for more festive, presumably social occasions. One Thanksgiving I had dinner at the Douglas house. It was stultifying. Nancy didn't say anything at all, and Douglas just talked about the lab all night."

Bill was apparently even less comfortable around women than he was around men. Sanders had the impression that there was something "asexual" about him. "There were plenty of women in our lab," he told me. "The lab had four female technicians, two female grad students, and a female postdoc. But as far as I know, Douglas never made any advances or innuendos, or even personal remarks, to any of them."

Why was he so aloof? The answer seems to lie in

his upbringing. Eleanor, his stolid, religious mother, with her job cleaning other people's homes and other people's squalid hotel rooms, brought him up strictly, laying great stress on propriety. Billy, his plumber father, wanted him to make something of himself. He was their only child, and he had been born late in his mother's life. They doted on him, but they demanded obedience; when he took liberties, they chastised him severely. He was expected to be quiet and unobtrusive around home, to keep himself and his room clean, to apply himself to his studies, to be polite to adults, and above all to avoid the kinds of activities to which other little boys, similarly disciplined, looked forward. Roughhousing. Hanging out. His parents felt that play was wasting time and that, in any event, when boys played together they just got into fights.

Perhaps their reasons were loving. Perhaps they were overly cautious about their son because he was their only child and there would never be another; doctors had warned the aging Mrs. Douglas not to attempt a second pregnancy. Perhaps they were overly strict because they yearned—for the boy's own good—to see him achieve a higher, more respected place in American society than theirs. Or perhaps they secretly disliked their son, wanted to crush his spirit. It can happen. Whatever their reasons, they overprotected and undersocialized the boy, placing upon him fierce demands for self-control and achievement. As a young child, Bill struggled hard to meet those demands, and when he transgressed and was punished, he apologized, made himself abject, promised he'd never be bad again. And eventually he learned to behave so well that his parents gave him the approving appellation "Little Man." But in light of his subsequent behavior, there is no doubt that behind his façade the "Little Man" was in much more turmoil than his parents knew, or wanted to know.

All through the spring of 1982, Bill played the "Little Man" role in relation to both his women. With Nancy he was uxorious, dependent, telephoning her several times a day to ask her opinion about a planned activity or to inquire whether there were any tasks she wanted him to perform on his way home. With Robin he was ingratiating, accommodating, always offering to help out with *her* domestic chores, to move furniture for her, to pick up her mail, to get broken objects repaired. And for a time it must have seemed to him that, cooperative and cajoling, he could handle having two women, could ride the crest of a secret affair without crashing to the shores of discovery and disgrace. Indeed, only one thing worried him in the beginning: he really didn't have the money to afford Robin. At least not for much longer. Within just a few months of his seeing her he'd gone through his and Nancy's entire personal savings, some $16,000. Then one day in the late spring it occurred to him that he might be able to get the money with which to swing the high cost of Robin Benedict. His grants entitled him to hire personnel. Why not employ Robin, put her on the payroll of some of his research projects at Tufts?

It was, he thought, a brainstorm of an idea. Robin had told him—as clearly so many of the girls at Good Time Charlie's tell their customers—that she was only going to be a hooker for a short time, just long enough to get some capital together. Then she was going to look for more respectable work. His willingness to believe her was part of his whole fantasy about her, his notion, not that she was a hooker with a heart of gold (even he knew that wasn't the case), but that she was a hooker with a golden brain. (He was so persuaded of her intellect that he eventually enrolled her in one of his scientific groups, the Tissue Culture Association, although there may have been vanity as well as admiration in this. He published scientific papers in the association's journal, *In Vitro*, and no doubt hoped she would read them, or at least notice them, and be impressed.) Therefore, putting Robin on the Tufts payroll seemed a solution to his dilemma that had advantages all around. Not only would it enable him to go on affording her, but it would bring her closer to him, give her an awareness of his importance in the scientific world, and start her out on her path toward respectability.

Soon thereafter, he sat down at his desk in the lab and wrote Robin a lengthy memo setting forth his plan. He would tell Tufts that she was working for him. Tufts would pay her for that work $200 a week, by university check, which would cover his first two-hour visits with her each week. He knew she might find it a nuisance to be paid by check, but in the end she might discover that it was in fact beneficial to earn money this way because it would legitimize her. "When you retire from 'business,'" he pontificated, "your résumé will not have a five-year gap."

Robin liked the scheme, and from that time forward, he claimed she was a graduate student from MIT whom he had hired to illustrate cell cultures.

The woman who had caught the fancy of the odd but respected professor was only twenty years old and had been out of high school for only two and a half years. But she was already well entrenched in prostitution. Robin Benedict had turned up in the Combat

Zone in the beginning of 1982. Almost immediately she came to the attention of the Boston Vice Squad. Detective Billy Dwyer spotted her on the street, told her to get moving (Boston permits solicitation only indoors, not out), and received a sharp, sarcastic response. "She was irritating, aggressive, too full of backtalk for her own good," he told me one night.

He and I were taking a tour of the Zone in Dwyer's unmarked car, his partner at the wheel. Dwyer, so intense that he conveys the sense of having banked but still-smoldering fires within, was talking to me over one shoulder, over the other keeping an eye out for any problems. From time to time he'd bark something at a hooker or a pimp—he knew them all—and they would startle and look uneasy. He shouted at a girl who seemed to be ogling a man across the street that she'd better get moving; at another, who'd just been released from jail on a robbery charge, that he wanted to see her release papers, so she'd better double-time it over to the car. Dwyer is known in the Zone as Billy the Driver, and everyone he shouted at complied with lightning speed. But apparently Robin hadn't. "She was one tough little number," Dwyer said. "The kind of girl you just knew would get into deep trouble. In fact, one day my boss said to her, 'Do you have any tattoos?' She snapped, 'Why?' And he told her, 'Just so that when we fish you out of the river—and I'll bet we have to someday—we'll know who you are.'"

Robin's parents described her differently. They maintained that, despite her line of work, she was sweet-tempered, a good girl, a devoted daughter.

Theirs was a cross-cultural marriage. Shirley Benedict, Robin's blond and buxom mother, grew up in Lawrence, Massachusetts. John Benedict, Robin's father, is a handsome Hispanic Trinidadian with high cheekbones and deeply set eyes that make him look like the sculptures of long-ago Amerindians. Color was an issue in the family. Robin indicated to friends, back in the days when she was in high school, that her father did not approve of her dating black men.

John was a commercial photographer employed by the Raytheon Corporation in Lawrence. Shirley worked as the manager of a jewelry store in a shopping mall there. The had five children—three boys and two girls. Robin was the fourth child and first daughter. This gave her a certain distinction; when she was born, her father hung a sheet across the front of the house, trained a slide projector on it, and displayed in majestic, magnified letters the message: "It's a girl!"

He had longed for a girl, and from the time she was an infant, he and this first daughter developed a special, exclusive attachment to one another. He said of Robin once, "I have five kids. But I just have one little girl." She said of him, "My daddy is *my* daddy." He shot thousands of pictures of her as she was growing up, and she early mastered a self-confident grin and a model's easy poise.

The Benedicts raised their children in Methuen, a small city in northern Massachusetts, near the New Hampshire border. In the early years of this century, it was a thriving milltown, attracting to its hilly streets a scrambled mix of immigrants. But eventually the mills shut down, and Methuen, like many New England towns, sank into lethargy. Unemployment grew severe, and crime flourished. Later, as a result of new high-tech plants, there was some economic revival, but there is still so much traffic in heroin and cocaine in the area that Lawrence—the town that borders Methuen and where Methuen teenagers go for high school—has an unusually high crime rate.

There are a handful of nice streets and houses in both Lawrence and Methuen. But for the most part, this is a region of dilapidated housing projects, rambling oversize Victorian houses that have begun to crumble and decay, and small ill-kept ranch houses on quarter-acre lots. Robin grew up in one such ranch house, a tiny green home with graying white shutters, which must have been cramped indeed when all five of the Benedict children were living there.

Still, the Benedicts managed. And they had fun as a family. John managed a marching group, the White Eagles Drum and Bugle Corps, and the children, carrying flags and brandishing shiny sabers, participated in holiday parades in the nearby New England towns. Summers, all the children went on vacation trips with their parents, and on holidays Shirley would dress the boys in suits and the girls in prim little coats with matching bonnets, and John would take their pictures.

In 1975 Robin entered the Greater Lawrence Regional Vocational Technical High School, known as the Voke. By then, she was a popular, fashion-conscious teenager who aspired to being voted her class's best-dressed member. She also had some artistic proclivities, according to one of her teachers, who said she was "one of the most talented people in the commercial art department."

She seemed, in those days, no different from other teenagers. She became a jogger, and whenever she felt she was gaining weight, she would put in extra time, running around a reservoir close to her house. She took up the flute, and whenever she felt dreamy or troubled, she would sit cross-legged on her bed and play, favoring in particular the sweet tunes of Barry Manilow and the urgent ones of Michael Jackson. She learned to drive, and her father taught her to crawl under the old Pinto to change the oil and keep the car in shape.

To look at photographs of Robin in those days is to see Everygirl: in a bouffant, off-the-shoulder dress for her Junior Prom; in a slinky, black spaghetti-strap number for the Senior Prom; playing the flute in the high school talent show; working on the yearbook with a camera slung around her neck.

But she must have found life dull. I was struck, as I wandered around Methuen inquiring into Robin's adolescence, by how little the town has to stimulate teenagers or to satisfy their longing for excitement and glamour. The main street is shabby. There are no lively gathering places. Teenage lovers drive to the Methuen Water Tower, a historic structure high on a hill, and stare at the view, daydreaming of places beyond Methuen. Or they neck in the one really private part of town, the Bellevue Cemetery. No wonder that in high school, Robin eventually began hanging out with a crowd of Hispanic teenagers from her school who knew where to find whatever action there was in the area. They would drive to discos in Manchester, New Hampshire, and Salisbury, Massachusetts, and Robin, who was light on her feet, would frequently win disco dance competitions. She also had her first sexual experiences. And, at around the time she was seventeen, an abortion.

One of Robin's high school boyfriends, a young man who eventually became an auto mechanic, remembered her from those days as "strong and smart," the kind of girl who was beautiful and knew it—and who knew as well that she wanted something more for herself than the life of a Methuen housewife.

One night during her senior year, Robin glimpsed a way to get the kind of life she daydreamed about. She had gone with a high school beau to attend a promotional football game that pitted the New England Patriots against the faculty of the Voke. After the game, there was a celebratory dinner, and Robin and her boyfriend got to talking with Ray Costic, a linebacker with the Patriots. Costic, a black from Mississippi, had been feeling out of place with many of the people he'd been meeting in New England, but he took a liking to Robin and her crowd and decided to join the group after dinner. They went to a disco and danced and drank, and Costic entertained the students with tales of his famous team, the places he'd been, the games he'd won. Robin found Costic, tall and muscular and far more worldly than the high school boys she was accustomed to dating, fascinating.

That summer, after graduation, she took a job at a small graphic arts company, and, although her parents had made it clear that they didn't want her dating black men, set her sights for Costic. He'd said he was lonely, so she invited him home. Her parents were football fans and, unaware of her romantic interest in the athlete, entertained him and politely. asked him to come again. He did and brought several of his teammates. Soon he was going to the Benedicts' regularly, enjoying Sunday dinners with them, getting them tickets to his games, driving them home afterward. But he made no move toward Robin. He knew that her father disapproved of him, and besides, he had a girlfriend back home in Mississippi, a woman who had borne him a child. But Robin didn't care about either of these facts and one lazy summer afternoon, while Ray was at one of her parents' back- yard barbecues, she cornered him in a foyer, declared her admiration, and kissed him ardently. Her passion overrode his reluctance, and not long afterward he invited her to live with him in his expensive and fash- ionably furnished apartment in Quincy, Massachu- setts.

Robin was "good in bed," Ray told reporters. But he liked her for her artistic abilities, too. Having decided to become an illustrator, she was taking some art courses at the prestigious Rhode Island School of De- sign. Costic was impressed with the skill with which she could draw his likeness and paint delicate oils of trees and flowers.

Ray "treats me like a queen," Robin told one of her former teachers. But she liked him for his way of life as well. That fall she traveled with him to all the Pa- triots' games, stayed in good hotels, went to a dizzy- ing round of glittering parties. She loved the fast track she was on, loved entering a crowded room with Ray and, the beauty and the ballplayer, being the center of attention. (One day, much later, there would be a rumor that she was a "mule" for former patriots, carrying in drugs for them. The Boston police re- ceived an anonymous tip that she was delivering co- caine to onetime players. But although she was investigated, no evidence to support the accusation was found and the investigation was dropped.)

She didn't, in those days, seem to let the admira- tion she increasingly received from men go to her head. She didn't seem to covet anyone's love but Ray's. She wanted him to marry her, and she tried to make herself indispensable, doing his cooking and cleaning and all his errands. And because it was important to him, she abandoned her own religion, Catholicism, and took instruction in his, the Jehovah's Witnesses. By the late fall of 1980, she even began going with the Witnesses as they knocked on doors, preaching the Gospel.

One night around Christmas 1980, Ray took Robin to a particularly lively party in the apartment of a friend of his in the housing complex. There were several prostitutes at the party, as well as a man Ray would later say he thought was a pimp, a short, compact, stern-looking black man with a fat diamond ring on his finger. The man, Clarence J. Rogers, whom everybody called "J.R.," kept staring at Robin. And at one point in the evening he observed to Ray, "That's the kind of child that you put out on the street."

If Ray became angry, he didn't indicate it. Perhaps he merely thought that the man, J.R., was a bad judge of character. After all, he knew Robin as a good girl, a decent girl. "Nice," "straight," were the adjectives he used about her.

But although she was so nice, so straight, at around that time he decided he didn't want to go on living with her. He felt an obligation to the woman back home in Mississippi who was the mother of his son. Reluctantly, but convinced he was doing the right thing, he told Robin that he was going back home to get married to his old girlfriend.

Robin felt cruelly abandoned. She cried. She pleaded with Ray not to leave her. And then she did an odd thing. Impulsively and recklessly, she telephoned Ray's hometown and, speaking with some of the Jehovah's Witnesses there, some of the very elders who would be performing the wedding, informed them that not only had the ballplayer been committing the sin of fornication with her, but he had been taking drugs with her as well.

Her attempts to hold on to her lover didn't work. If anything, those attempts, smacking as they did of emotional blackmail, made Ray surer than ever that he wanted to leave her. Ignoring her tears, he went back south and got married.

She was different after that. Depressed and disheartened, she continued for a while to take religious instruction, but soon she began telling her instructors that she was also taking drugs. Shortly she stopped attending Witness meetings altogether. She was still working at the graphic arts company, but soon her coworkers began to notice that when she left work, she didn't go home alone anymore. She was picked up by a black man driving a brand-new Mercedes.

Some of her friends in the eight-person office, a place so small it was difficult to keep a secret, kept asking her about him. But Robin wouldn't say a word about the man with the Mercedes or about what he did for a living. Her boss, suspecting he might be involved in some kind of illegal occupation, advised her not to see him, but Robin paid no attention. "She didn't want to hear it," her boss said.

He and her other friends at work kept badgering her about her new relationship, and one day Robin just upped and quit her job and said she was going to California. Her friends didn't see her around anymore.

Late in 1981, Ray Costic had a change of heart about Robin. His little son had been killed in a motel fire in Florida, and he and his wife were fighting all the time. Still down south, he began thinking nostalgically about his former girlfriend, and he asked some of his old Patriot friends what she was up to. She was seeing J.R., they informed him.

Ray called Robin's mother and tried to get her telephone number. But Shirley Benedict wouldn't give it to him, not even when he told her he thought J.R. was a pimp. Finally, friends got him a number for her at an apartment she was sharing with J.R., Savi Bisram, and Savi's two-year-old son, Taj—whose father was J.R. This odd extended family was living in the suburbs of Boston.

Robin was abrupt with Ray. She told him that she didn't "need any more men friends."

Shortly afterward, he heard that she had been seen working in the Combat Zone. He asked a mutual friend to go there and check out the rumor. The friend went, saw Robin, and tried to speak with her. She pretended she didn't know him.

By then she was making $1,000 a night. And soon she would meet Bill Douglas, and would once again —for a short time, at least—be treated like a queen.

Throughout the spring and early summer of 1982, Douglas's infatuation with Robin grew. But if he was high on love, he was often high on something else, too. One night, about a month and a half after he started seeing her, Robin introduced him to cocaine. She herself was a steady user; from the beginning, he had been paying for her supply. Now he began to pay for his own supply as well, and often, when they met late at night, they would do the drug together. Robin, he would eventually tell the police, using words a child might use to describe a mother's grooming, "was very strict" about their habit and "would always check her nose and my nose very thoroughly because she didn't want to go back to the bar and have anyone see any traces."

In this and other ways, Douglas found himself drawn deeper and deeper into Robin's world. He loved it. He met two other young prostitutes with whom she shared the Beacon Street trick pad and got to know them, talking to them about their lives and why they had gone into the business of sex. He studied the culture of Robin and her friends as he might study a new scientific field, noticing small details, learning the lingo, calling the prostitutes by the term they themselves used—"working girls"—and remembering with fascination such tidbits as the fact that one of Robin's girlfriends only liked driving red cars and that some prostitutes, Robin among them, were too fastidious to sleep where they worked.

He didn't know that Robin had a pimp—at least, not in those glory days. What was on his mind then was simply being able to spend as much time with her as he could. And he began to see her, not just at night, but in the afternoons before she started hustling, meeting her for a meal at a nearby Howard Johnson's. He also changed his schedule at Tufts, arranging to do his research in the truly small hours of the morning so that he could stay in his lab until she finished her work. He didn't care that this was often not until 2:30 A.M. or even later. Whenever she finished, he would go to her and often stay with her until 4 or 5 A.M. What he wanted was to be the last man she saw at night and to be with her every night.

He called her "Treasure." He called her "Precious Lady." And he began to shower her with gifts. Money. Records. Clothes. One night he even invented a delicious game of grab bag. He filled an envelope with slips of paper, on which he named various treats, and let her pull out a slip before they made love. She had long, tapered nails that she loved to keep exquisitely manicured, and he wrote on one of the slips: "Nails by Dorothy as often as you want them!" She had thick, flowing hair that needed constant attention, and he wrote on another slip: "A hair permanent at a salon of your choice as often as you wish!" On another slip he offered: "One complete set of super expensive cosmetics of your choice!" On another, "One bike of your choice!" It was the kind of game a father, used to the entertainments at children's parties, would have devised.

In his letters, now, he was using a coy lovers' code. He'd end his epistles with "QH's," meaning "quick hugs," and tell Robin how much he longed for "Vela-mint transfers"—the exchange, his lips to her, of the little mint candies. And he'd draw cartoons on the bottom of his notes, the way adolescents do, round moonfaces of himself downcast followed by a plus sign and Robin's face. The sad Douglas face, plus the face of Robin, equaled, he drew, a happy Douglas face.

But if for the most part the letters were childish, the sentiments banal, there was some indication that in some small way, the emotionally stunted professor was at last beginning to experience an authentic romantic attachment. Once in a while, here and there, he would write of love not just in abstractions and clichés, but he would fleetingly describe personal experiences, particularized disappointments or triumphs. And when he did, he seemed to be on the verge of finding an individual, private voice for his feelings.

In May, when he was on a trip to Saskatoon, he wrote Robin that he sorely missed her and his children, implying that the affection he bore toward each was equal. He also—sounding like any married man carrying on an adulterous affair—complained about the difficulties of arranging time with his sweetheart. "My lab group at Tufts had a cookout for one of my postdoctoral fellows.... I wanted to ask you if you could go with me to this party... but Nancy would not tell me until the last minute if she was going or not (she did not) and I did not want to ask you at the last minute. Next lab party I am just going to ask you and not tell her about the party." Rather touchingly, he described an accolade he'd received at the cookout, as if to hint to Robin that despite his drawbacks, he was not an altogether unworthy man. "One of my graduate students," he wrote, boasting ever so indirectly, "showed up in a sweatshirt. On the front of the shirt was the skyline of Boston with many of the skyscrapers. Across the buildings was written in large capital letters—WHJD—. [The graduate student] suggested that all lab members in William Henry James Douglas's lab get one."

At last, in the summer of 1982, he started to lose weight. "He did it on the strangest diet you ever saw," one of his colleagues told me. "He went on eating all the stuff he liked—hot dogs, cheese and crackers, ice cream, cookies. And he even drank beer. But he lost a lot of weight. I figure he was taking Benzedrine." No matter. Robin had told him he was gross, and in an effort to please her he began to shed the cage of fat that had for years imprisoned him.

Darkness Within

Being in love is never a simple matter. But for a man like a professor, always constrained, always interested in maintaining appearances, being in love was particularly complex. A part of him balked at adoring Robin. A part of him despised himself for it.

One night in the fall of 1982 this self-hatred surfaced, was articulated. But no one, not even Douglas himself, recognized its symptoms or understood the frightening future the words foreboded. That night he'd arranged, as was his habit, to be Robin's last date, the lover she saw when she was finished with all her other johns, the man she came home to after work, so to speak. He occupied himself in his lab at Tufts, waiting for her to telephone and say that she was free, and when she did, he hurried to her. They made love. He gave her $100. And afterward they left her trick pad, a new one she had just rented, and, in the cool, crisp dawn, went for a stroll.

They were just past Robin's building when suddenly the young woman, her arm tucked familiarly into Douglas's, noticed Detective Dwyer's car parked just down the street. "Maybe they won't notice us," she said. "Let's keep walking." But she warned Douglas that if they were noticed, and if the police

detained them, he should not under any circumstances reveal that he had given her money. If he
didn't admit to having paid her, she might be ha-
rassed but she couldn't be arrested. "No matter how
hard they press you," Robin coached him, "just don't
say anything about money."

They continued walking, trying to stay calm, but
seconds later Dwyer and his partner, Mark Malloy,
leaped out of the car. Dwyer took Robin aside and
Malloy began interrogating Douglas. "Are you married?" he asked.

Douglas said he was, and Malloy said, "Well, this is
going to make a nice stink in the papers, isn't it?"

Douglas began to shake.

"How much money did you give her?" Malloy demanded.

He forced himself to say "None," and he even
maintained that Robin worked for him over at the
medical school and couldn't possibly be a prostitute.

He was proud of himself, then, and prouder still
when Dwyer, too, began to press him. He didn't cave
in, not even when Dwyer said, "Come on, we know
you were in that apartment with her," and insisted on
taking him and Robin back to it.

There, Dwyer looked the apartment over and, certain of the purpose for which Robin was using it, told
her she would have to move out of this place, too.
Then he told Douglas to wise up. Robin was not only
a hooker, he informed him, but she had a pimp.
"Every cent you give her is going to her pimp," he
said.

Douglas refused to believe him. "You don't know
what you're talking about," he said.

"Oh, I don't, huh?" Dwyer got out a photograph

and tried to show it to him. He wouldn't look at it. Then Dwyer uttered a name, Clarence J. Rogers. That was Robin's pimp, he said. But Douglas just kept repeating that it was impossible and that Robin wasn't even a prostitute. Maybe they had her mixed up with someone else.

Much later Dwyer would say, "He was adamant. He wouldn't budge. I think he didn't want to know she had a pimp. I mean, she just ran roughshod over him and he just followed her around, like she had him by the nose. . . . He was totally, totally infatuated."

It certainly looked that way. But infatuation was only one of the emotions that Douglas harbored toward Robin. It would turn out that he himself was responsible for Malloy and Dwyer's having parked on Marlborough Street at that time on that night. It would turn out that just before leaving Tufts to be with Robin, he had telephoned the police and made a complaint about the trafficking in prostitution that was going on in her building. Disguising his voice, he had said to the officer who answered the phone that prostitutes working out of the building were ruining the neighborhood. "Bringing in undesirable elements" were the words he used. And before he hung up, he insisted, "I want it stopped."

By then, Douglas had ample reason to resent Robin, who was costing him so much money. But in fact, although no one knew it at the time, he had been surreptitiously calling her activities to the attention of the police from the very first days of his involvement with her. And as a result Robin, from those very first days, kept getting arrested.

Douglas brought about her first arrest just weeks after they started seeing one another. He notified the police that she was with a john in her car. They came careening after her in a vice squad vehicle and, establishing that she'd solicited the fellow, a young music student, hauled them both down to court. Soon afterward she was arrested a second time. And a third. And a fourth. Other working girls didn't get arrested so frequently, she'd complain to Douglas, who would listen, sympathetic and consoling, never acknowledging his role in the proceedings.

Why would a man seek to get the woman with whom he was infatuated in trouble with the police? Detective Dwyer, discussing the matter with me months after it had been discovered, said, "Most likely, Douglas wanted to see Robin busted because he was jealous of the other men she saw and figured that if she kept getting arrested, she'd have to give up prostitution. Then she'd be his alone." But Dwyer, a straightforward, reasonable man, was seeking a rational explanation for something that was far from rational. He failed to fathom Douglas's tortured, complex personality. Not that it is easy to do. It would take someone as attuned to the darkness within the human soul as Dostoyevsky, who wrote in *Notes From the Underground*, the story of an intellectual who falls in love with a prostitute, that he tormented himself with the question, "Should I not begin to hate her, perhaps, even tomorrow, just because I had kissed her feet today?"

William Douglas, by the fall of 1982, had come to hate himself, to view himself, in his own words, as an "undesirable element." But he had also, virtually from the day he fell in love with Robin—from the first day he had, so to speak, kissed her feet—begun to hate her.

* * *

To be on the receiving end of obsessive love can be flattering, at least at first. Thus, it is often only after a long while that, when courted by an obsessive lover, even a mature and sophisticated woman recognizes the threat implicit in such love. Robin was only twenty and, while sexually wise beyond her years, still relatively inexperienced romantically. All through the early months of her relationship with Douglas, she not only didn't know he was causing her arrests, but had no comprehension of the complexity of his feelings toward himself or toward her. Emotionally naive, she had no inkling that he loved her in any but a unidimensional, storybook way. Moreover, she was vain and believed herself entitled to love. Small wonder, then, that although she was cynical in her own behavior, she imagined others as sincere, as feeling exactly what they said they felt. She saw proof of Douglas's fond feelings in his generosity. One day she wanted a MasterCard, and he willingly lied to bank officials, saying she was his employee, so she could get one. Another time she wanted a safe place to stash her cocaine, so he rented a safety deposit box in both their names. And when she needed a new car, he bought her the very one she coveted—a silver Toyota Starlet. Star was the name many pimps gave their most lucrative girls, but she didn't tell Douglas this.

She found proof of his devotion in other ways, too. He was always willing to help her out, to carry her belongings whenever she had to move, to pick up her mail at the post office box she maintained, to go to court and lend her moral support whenever she got arrested. One time when he came he vouched for her, telling the judge, just as he had told Dwyer and Malloy, that it was preposterous for anyone to call her a prostitute since she made her living by doing scientific illustrations for him at the medical school.

But if Robin lacked the sophistication, the imagination, or the desire, to see Douglas's ambivalence toward her, she nevertheless was aware that he was not altogether easy to control. There was an irritating, infantile side to him that she couldn't quite cope with. For one thing, he couldn't take no for an answer; when she'd tell him she was too busy to see him, he'd telephone her a dozen times to beg and plead with her to change her mind. For another, he couldn't keep his mouth shut, at least around her friends; she'd warned him not to say a word about their drug habit, but he began talking about it to the girls at Good Time Charlie's.

She'd lash out at him for these transgressions, read him the riot act. But he'd go all babyish on her and apologize and beg for forgiveness, swearing he would never give her any trouble again and saying he loved her more than he'd ever loved anyone in his whole long life. Adulated—if annoyed—she would accept his apologies.

In the fall of 1982, Douglas's colleagues in the Tufts Anatomy and Cellular Biology Department began whispering about him. It doesn't take much to get the members of an academic department gossiping. Personalities and peccadillos preoccupy academicians because, for all the intellectual territory over which their minds roam, the world they actually occupy is so sealed off, so hermetic, that they might as well live in tiny towns. Moreover, in the case of William Douglas, it was hard for his colleagues not to gossip. For one thing, he had lost so much weight that his clothes

hung from him. For another, he was behaving uncharacteristically. He almost never came into the lab
in the daytime hours anymore. He kept missing appointments with students. He didn't turn up at departmental meetings and laboratory supervisory
sessions. And on the rare occasions that a department
member spotted him, he seemed more jumpy and ill
at ease than usual.

At first his colleagues thought simply that the repressed professor had at last broken out and was having an affair, and they joked about the matter.
Douglas had mentioned to one of them a while back,
and she had told the others, that if a Robin Benedict
telephoned, he was to be called to the phone no matter what he was doing, whether he was in the midst
of a crucial experiment or in an important meeting.
Benedict, he had explained, was a graduate student
who was working with him on a research project at
MIT. Perhaps, his colleagues laughed, Douglas was
having an affair with this uniquely favored student.

But Professor Sanders and Jane Aghajanian, the
chief technician in the lab, soon began to suspect
something more sinister. One day, during a routine
check of the financial records of the projects on
which they worked with Douglas, they discovered
that their lab head had been submitting expense
vouchers for surprisingly large amounts of money
against university grants shared by all of them. More
important, the expenses he claimed to have incurred
made little sense. He had submitted vouchers for
trips abroad when, as far as they knew, he hadn't
been away, vouchers for the entertainment and lodg-
ing of visiting scientists they had never seen, and
vouchers for work performed by the Benedict "gradu-

ate student," who had never even put in an appearance in the lab.

Sanders and Aghajanian brought the puzzling expenses to the attention of the Tufts auditing department. The auditors noticed some discrepancies and launched a discreet investigation.

Douglas may have suspected he was under investigation, but he didn't stop stealing from his grants. Some of the scams and swindles he undertook were ludicrous. He hired Robin as a consultant on a project to develop a computer program for analyzing prostate tissue. He requisitioned from a medical supply house used by Tufts Medical School what he described on a voucher as "fluid collection units," which turned out to be condoms that Robin, on the nights business was bad, sold to other Combat Zone hookers at a handsome profit. He added Savi Bisram's name to the list of people he was employing for research, and Tufts issued her a check for $9,000. (Savi cashed the check and turned the money over to Robin.) He gave Robin herself some $20,000 directly. And he submitted numerous other false vouchers for money supposedly spent by himself. Ultimately, he swindled some $67,000 from Tufts within the space of a year. And virtually all this money he gave to Robin.

She spent it freely, lavishing her income on designer clothes, furs, soft leather boots, necklaces worth thousands of dollars apiece. She also spent it on cocaine. She had become, at twenty, a girl without a future, a child-woman who reveled in flattery, fripperies, and the fun of the moment. Sometimes she'd go home to Methuen, where her parents had hung many of her sketches and paintings throughout the house. She'd study them, talk about continuing her art education. But according to a prostitute who knew her, when they'd first met, Robin had frequently mentioned that she hoped one day to make her living by drawing, but by the fall of 1982 she no longer took seriously the possibility of becoming an artist. "There were lots of reasons," the prostitute said. "The cut in pay, for one."

Sometime in October Douglas was officially informed that he was suspected of having padded his expense accounts. He was called to a meeting by Richard Thorngren, the comptroller of Tufts, and Steven Manos, a vice president of the university, shown his questionable vouchers, and asked to justify them. Had he attended the out-of-town meetings he said he had? What kind of work had Benedict and Bisram performed?

He stayed calm at first. He began leafing methodically through his appointment calendar. But, of course, there were no entries for the trips, and after a while he admitted that some of his vouchers were "problems and false." Still, he insisted that some of the others being questioned were valid. And he particularly maintained that the vouchers for money paid to Benedict and Bisram were on the up and up.

Thorngren contemplated Douglas and then, informing him that he was going to launch a full-scale investigation, demanded to speak with Robin Benedict and Savi Bisram. Douglas grew agitated and confused. The vouchers for the women's work were valid, he repeated. But if they weren't, he added brightly, and if it turned out he owed the university money, why, he'd pay it right back. It was as if he believed that all he needed to do was make restitution, and apologize, and the matter would be forgiven and forgotten.

That same month, Nancy Douglas, too, demanded an accounting from Bill. This was unusual for her. For years he had been absenting himself from the household in the middle of the night, but always she had chosen to accept his explanation that he kept his extraordinary hours because his experiments were so delicate, so important, that they required round-the-clock attention.

I thought when I first heard how trusting she'd always been that Nancy must be an extremely naive woman. But on reflection I recalled that I had known many women, and even some men as well, who ignored even the most telling evidence of sexual disloyalty, who appeared almost to prefer to look the other way so as to deny their spouse's infidelities. To accomplish this, they generally convinced themselves that the spouse was unusually worthwhile—a talent, a prodigy, a fantastic father, a magnificent mother, a superb provider. I was to learn that Nancy took the tack that Bill was a genius—an eccentric one, perhaps, but nevertheless a genius. There are many marriages in which there is a star and a supporting cast. The Douglases' marriage seems to have been one of them.

In such marriages, the star is not just coddled but excused. In this case, no matter what Nancy found out about her husband—that he was having an affair with another woman, that he was in love with that woman—she would lay the blame for his actions, not on him, but on someone or something else. At fault were the pressures of academic life, Bill's demanding supervisors at Tufts, or even, poor woman, herself.

She was Bill's fan, and never—at least in the public eye—did she waver from that role.

But although she may not have blamed Bill for it, by October 1982 Nancy Douglas had at last become unable to hide from herself the probability that he was seeing another woman. Characteristically, she believed that if she hadn't taken a night job, he might not have been unfaithful. But no matter whose fault it was, she felt she needed to know what was going on, and she confronted Bill with her fears.

What happened next was typical of their marriage —and, I suppose, of many marriages. Bill, apologizing profusely, told her about his girlfriend and asked Nancy if she wanted a divorce. She said no, not if they could patch things up. Bill said they could and promised her that from now on he'd stop seeing Robin and try to spend more time at home. And although he assured her that none of it was her fault, Nancy promised Bill that from now on she would no longer work nights.

She kept her end of the bargain, but Bill didn't keep his. He went on seeing Robin. And one night, in a burst of misery, Nancy penned a kind of diary entry to herself, pouring out her problems on paper. "Why is this happening? Why won't he just come home?" she wrote. "I think he's on drugs, too. Oh, God. Please help me. Please, please help me. I can't take any more."

While Nancy was bemoaning her fate, the Tufts investigation was deepening. But Douglas kept stalling the examiners about bringing in Robin and Savi. And, curiously, though he now knew for certain that his expenses were being scrutinized, in November he submitted a bill for $3,597 for graphic work performed by Robin.

What possessed him to go on with the deceit once he had been warned he was being watched? Perhaps cocaine had scrambled his brain. The drug produces euphoria, a sense of invulnerability, and the conviction that the mores of the rest of the world need not govern one's own behavior. No doubt, too, the fact that his career was now in jeopardy because of Robin may have strengthened his resolve to hold on to her; if he couldn't have her, then what had it all been for? However, there was no way to see Robin without paying for the privilege. And so he paid, and continued to pay.

But he had always felt subjugated by his passion for her, and a change began to come over him. He became resentful. He didn't let on to Robin that it angered him to keep having to fork over money to her. He gave her whatever she asked. But increasingly he would spitefully, passive-aggressively, get even with her by going behind her back.

One night in November, she'd been irritable throughout the latest costly hour they'd spent together, and nothing he'd done or said had helped to alleviate her mood. They had argued the whole time. Yet, at the end of the hour, she had demanded her usual fee. It made him furious and later, after he'd left her, he decided to get even with her by breaking into her apartment and stealing from her. "What upset me," he would eventually explain, was that "I ended up paying for the hour, but it really bothered me because I didn't feel that that was right."

Her place at this time was on Commonwealth Avenue, the apartment to which she moved after Dwyer forced her to vacate her Marlborough Street pad. At the time of the move, Robin had asked Douglas to assist her, and he'd rented the U-Haul and done the driving and unloading. Another bit of help she'd asked of him was that he go to a locksmith's and get several sets of keys made for her. He'd done that, too. But without her permission or knowledge, he'd had an extra set made for himself.

On the night in question, he returned to the building after his quarrelsome hour with Robin and, parking his car outside, lurked there, studying her comings and goings. He saw her go in with a john, come out a while later, get into her car, drive off, and return with a new man. Every half hour or hour she'd leave, drive away, and return in some twelve to twenty minutes. Her routine would, he realized, give him just enough time to stage a robbery.

He'd done it before. He'd staged a break-in at her old apartment. There, he'd crept around to the back of the building, broken a pane in the rear door to gain entry, and then stolen Robin's telephones and an answering machine he'd bought her as a present, careful to scatter her other possessions around so that it would look like a regular robbery.

This time, on Commonwealth Avenue, it was going to be a lot easier. He wouldn't have to risk arousing the neighbors by breaking any glass. He had the keys, so he'd just let himself in. And this time he'd steal cash, not just electronic equipment. She loved money, and its loss would really annoy her, he thought. And besides, if he took money, the robbery would truly seem authentic.

He waited until she left on one of her forays back to Good Time Charlie's. Then, stealthily, he let himself into her apartment and stole $300 as well as the new answering machine he'd given her to replace the old one. But while he took cash and the phone machine, he also made off with something no bona fide robber would have. He pocketed her little red address book, with the names and phone numbers of most of her clients.

Robin, returning from Good Time Charlie's, a client nuzzling her neck, arrived home to chaos. Always edgy and prone to hysteria, she flew into a tantrum, began to sob and rage, told Douglas for weeks afterward how violated she'd felt by the weirdo who'd ripped her off. He agreed that the robber was a "freak." He agreed so heartily that although J.R. suspected the robber might have been the professor himself, Robin said she didn't think so.

Perhaps she didn't want to know. By now, she had a veritable passion for money, and Douglas was her most reliable source. He had given her so much money, so many gifts, and now he was promising to help her buy the one thing she desired above all others—a house of her own. She'd wanted one ever since she'd been a little girl in Methuen, sharing a bedroom with her sister, squeezing into the tiny dining alcove with her parents, her sister, and her three brothers. J.R., who was still her constant companion, thought she should cut the professor loose, but she ignored his advice and went on seeing him.

In the next few weeks, Bill learned things about Robin he hadn't known, or at least fully accepted, before. Armed with her address book, he learned about all her numerous clients, and listening to the messages on her phone machine, in particular an affectionate one she'd left for J.R., he at last realized that she had a pimp.

The discovery enraged him. He had acquiesced to

all her demands, albeit while going behind her back to get even. He had been willing to satisfy his passion under any terms. Terms were par for her profession. But that there was another man in her life, a man to whom she gave herself freely, changed the whole picture. Previously, he'd refused even to consider that there might be such a man. But now he could no longer deny this truth to himself, and anger began to boil up in him.

Robin's behavior didn't help the situation. Early in December, she took $25,000, which she had obtained from Douglas, and placed a down payment on a two-story wooden house on a shabby but respectable lower-middle-class street in Malden, Massachusetts. A local bank had given her a mortgage for another $25,000 and overnight she was a property owner, a woman of substance. She owed that new definition of herself to Douglas. But when, a few days later, he asked her where the house was, she said, "I don't want you to know where it is." She knew all about the Tufts investigation by then, knew that the source of his largesse might soon dry up, and the knowledge made her cavalier. "I don't want you to have my home phone number," she said to end the conversation.

With the house an accomplished fact, by the end of the month Robin seemed, at least temporarily, to have decided to take J.R.'s advice and extricate herself from the professor's attentions. On New Year's Eve, he begged her for a date, even a short date, but she told him she was busy. That evening he telephoned her at the apartment in Natick, where she and J.R. were still living, imploring her at least to talk with him on that most romantic of all nights. Robin listened to him for a while, but then she cut him off.

"I've got to go," she snapped. "We're leaving in a few minutes." She slammed the phone down hard.

This time her rejection suited Douglas. He'd told her he was speaking to her from Boston, but in fact he had called her from across the street from the apartment. Now, from her words when she hung up on him, he realized that he might, at long last, be able to lay eyes on the man she was living with. Was the man black or white? Short or tall? Slight? Powerful? He wanted desperately to know and, getting into his car, waited for her and whomever she'd meant by "we" to emerge. She'd said they would be leaving in a few minutes. Excited, he sat tensely behind the wheel.

But no one came out of her building. He waited and waited. It was a cold night, but he was wearing a fleece-lined coat, so he just sat still and waited some more. He sat in the darkened car for an hour. And then another hour. But although he remained in the car for much of the night, Robin never emerged.

At last, deeply frustrated, he decided she must have seen him sitting there.

Perhaps she had, for the next day she telephoned and told him in no uncertain words how little she thought of him. He was a pest and a nag, she said. He was stupid. He made her so angry that she didn't want to hear from him at all, at least not until she got over her anger.

Her repudiation was like a hammer blow to him. How could he live without speaking to her? Still, he knew she was right. He *had* been a pest and a nag. He would mend his ways, and then surely she would speak with him again. Sitting down with a sheaf of paper in front of him, he began to write to her. He wrote her an abject, sorrowful letter. "You know I am sad that it happened but I have only myself to blame," he scrawled. "I will change my ways! I will work hard on trying to act like an adult when I interact with you and not some lovestruck teenager. I must learn to think through a situation clearly before acting and not be a pest or a nag. During the time we are apart I will work hard on these problem areas to correct the defects."

He told her he admired her for her smile, and how he loved squeezing her hand, and how grateful he was for "You being You You You You You."

And he told her about a touching childhood longing: "Dear, when I was a teenager growing up I used to dream about designing a machine that would reverse time and let you relive time and places that you have already had. I guess all kids have thoughts like that. Today I wish I was clever enough to make one of those instruments for two reasons. For one reason, to go back in time and change the stupid things I did, and do it right. . . . The second reason is to act the appropriate way when I am with you, so that I could be someone you are proud of, someone that you respect, someone that you care to be with."

Twilight of the Affair

That January the New England air was crystal clear and the Douglas children got out their sleds and skates. Pammy had become a first-rate figure skater, and Bill could see, in her spirited pirouettes on the ice, a reflection of the best side of himself, a reaping of grace from the years in which he had shuttled her back and forth to her skating lessons. But it gave him no pleasure. Nor did his sons' accomplishments on the computer he'd gotten for them. The children were so much more adjusted than he had been as a teenager. They had friends, made sleepover dates. Billy was even a halfback on the high school football team. All of this should have comforted him. But he was still being investigated by Tufts. His career was crumbling. And Robin, for whom he'd risked that career, was still refusing to see or speak with him. He began to grow depressed.

Robin, for her part, had moved with J.R. to the new house and was fixing it up, making it truly the house of her dreams. She shopped for fabric, interviewed carpenters, selected appliances. And because she'd been having so much trouble with the police in Boston, she and J.R. agreed she should give up the city for a time and get some work in the suburbs. She took a job as a masseuse in a health club in Saugus, some ten miles from Malden, and devoted herself, when she wasn't working, to the renovations. For a brief while she was happy. For a brief while she may even have imagined herself to be once again the girl with great expectations she'd been in the early days of her love affair with Costic.

The neighbors on Cliff Street, all whites, felt disconcerted when they first saw J.R. I talked to several people who insisted that they had nothing against black people moving onto the street but that J.R. had worried them. He wasn't your ordinary black man, they said. He dressed outrageously. He wore purple pants and a black fur jacket. And while everyone else on the street had American cars or, at the most exotic, Japanese makes, J.R. drove a red Audi. They didn't want me to think they were prejudiced, they said, but J.R. would have made anybody nervous.

Interestingly, however, they soon accepted J.R.'s presence on their block. Or so they said. One neighbor told me that the presence of the Hispanic-looking but conservatively dressed Robin at J.R.'s side was the reassuring factor. Another said that what assuaged the neighborhood was the way the new people launched into making substantial improvements to their property. They gutted the kitchen and purchased new equipment. They ripped out walls; they even installed a skylight. Said this neighbor, "We began to accept them, because it looked as if they were going to turn out to be as house-proud and middle class as everyone else on the street."

But if the neighbors were reassured, Robin and J.R. weren't altogether content at their new address. Despite Robin's refusal to give it to Douglas, he'd ferreted it out, and now sometimes they'd see his Toyota

—a twin of hers—parked just across the street. And he kept on writing to her at her post office number and leaving messages for her at her answering service and, once she began working at the health club, trying to make appointments with her there.

One day in early January, hoping to throw him off her scent, she called him and left a message that she was no longer working at the club.

Douglas was desperate to find out if it was true. Shortly after getting her message, he drove to a motel in the vicinity of the Danish Health Club. Behind the motel was a forested, snowy hill from which the club was visible. Taking a pair of binoculars, he climbed up among the trees and, hidden, waited to see if Robin's car would turn up at the club. When it did, he knew she was lying to him and his spirits plunged even lower.

But the worst was still to come. On January 11, he was once again called to a meeting at Tufts on the matter of his expenses. This time he was informed that the auditors now knew for certain that he had been stealing from his grants. He was asked for his resignation. He had no choice but to give it.

The following day he turned up at his laboratory to collect his research and personal possessions. But he was denied entry. And the chairman of Anatomy and Cellular Biology, a woman who had sought him out six years earlier because she had the highest respect for his research and believed he would round out the department, came and escorted him off the premises. He stood at the elevator saying goodbye to her, and even as he did so locksmiths arrived and changed the locks on his office and laboratory.

In his desk drawer, never to be retrieved by him, were two eight-by-ten photographs of drawings Robin had done. One was a picture of three flowers, and on its back was the inscription: "To my favorite Prof. Talk to you later. Robin. 8/11/82." The other depicted a pretty girl surrounded by four natty men in tuxedos. On the back of this one was the message: "To my favorite professor. I signed [this] while we were sitting in my home in Natick on November 18, 1982. A moment I do believe you will treasure for quite some time. (Me too.) You can never tell what we are going to do next. It's been wonderful and will be more wonderful in times to come. Let's enjoy them. Always, Robin."

He thought about her constantly in the next few days, and on January 14 he wrote to her, pouring out his loneliness and his disgrace. "I need your help!" he wrote. "I am so depressed and sad. Everything in my life is going wrong lately. I truly need a friend that I can talk with and share things with."

The letter went unanswered. And on January 21 he went back to Saugus and, concealed among the trees high up on the hill behind the motel, spied on her once again. There was her Toyota, which he'd paid for, in the health club parking lot. He made up his mind to get even with her for turning her back on him after all he'd done for her, lost for her. But how?

The idea came to him a moment later. As he was leaving the hill, he noticed a billboard with the name and telephone number of a man selling garage doors, a Mr. Schloss. He went to a telephone booth and, dialing the Saugus Board of Health, asked for the health commissioner. When Joseph Tabbi, health agent for the town of Saugus, got on the wire, he said in a high falsetto, "My name is Mr. Schloss. I'm on the road a lot. I'm a salesman." And he then proceeded to inform Tabbi that over at the Danish Health Club, there was a woman who claimed to be a masseuse but who was really a prostitute. "The woman is there in the club, now," he complained. "You've got to do something about it."

The health agent said he'd send someone right over.

Douglas drove to a restaurant that had a good view of the Danish Health Club. He asked the waitress to give him a window table. He ordered food and toyed with it nervously, looking out the window until he saw a car pull up at the club and a man with a harried expression and businesslike gait go inside. A few minutes later the man reappeared, this time with the manager of the club. The two walked around to the back of the building, deep in serious conversation. He saw them look at Robin's car. Then the men went back inside, and a few minutes later Robin came out, carrying her bag. Moments later she left the Danish Health Club parking lot, never to return. She too had been fired. And he had engineered—and even gotten to witness—the whole humiliating scene.

If Douglas was pleased with himself at the time, afterward he found that his revenge gave him little satisfaction. Despite his fury at Robin, he still wanted to see her. But whenever he managed to reach her, she said they were finished.

He refused to believe her and held long dialogues with himself in which he consoled himself with the thought that surely one of these days she'd make up with him. Hadn't she said once that she'd learned forgiveness in the bosom of her family? Hadn't she told him all about how she'd had an uncle who'd stolen money from her parents and landed in jail but been forgiven by the family, who'd even gone to visit him? Anyway, Robin would no doubt make up with him *someday* because even when she'd been angriest, she'd never said, "I will *never* see you again." It was one of the things he treasured most about her. And besides, there was something else that gave him hope. It was the way she liked money. He figured her passion for money was particularly related to her passion for cocaine. And if only he could get another job, if only he could offer her the money with which to indulge her habit, surely he'd be able to persuade her to see him again.

His musings proved right. Several weeks later, the State University of New York in Plattsburgh, his old stamping ground, came through with a job offer. He'd sent out feelers to SUNY shortly after the Tufts investigation had begun and now, unaware of the scandal, they promised him a professorship, starting in September, and invited him to come to Plattsburgh immediately to codirect a week-long seminar in tissue culture. Taking heart, he called Robin and asked her to accompany him. And, his good fortune making him euphoric and expansive, he promised her that if she would come, he'd pay her $1,000 a day.

Robin said yes. How could she, why would she, when by now she knew that Douglas was shadowing her, even if she didn't know he was behind her arrests and the health club firing? The answer was in part Robin's greed. Just as Douglas had suspected, when offered enough money, she could readily put anger aside. But apparently she also, like many beautiful women, believed that because an admirer said he loved her, he truly did, and that this meant he would never hurt her, that she would always be the person in control of the relationship. On February 17, the next to the last day of the seminar, she flew to Plattsburgh.

Bill met her at the airport, and they spent the night together. The following morning she accompanied him to the last sessions of the seminar. He was overjoyed, his troubles forgotten, at least for the moment. He was back in the city in which he had gone to college, been a nobody, a shy youth with no prospects. Now he had just finished directing a highly esoteric conference on the subject of tissue culture. He was surrounded by the leading lights in his field, scholars who were exploring the very farthest edges of the mysteries of biology, creating life in glass dishes, playing God. And he was there with Robin, his Galatea. That morning, during a break in the formal part of the seminar, he introduced her to his colleagues. Completely immersed in fantasy, he pretended to his peers and perhaps even to himself that she was not the tawdry, drug-dependent hooker from the Combat Zone who went down on strangers in the back of their cars, but a classy, brilliant young scientist, the kind of girlfriend he had always longed for. He told his colleagues she was his graduate student, one of his brightest. That's why he'd brought her.

Several of his colleagues tried to make conversation with her that day. One probed her about her goals. What were her major interests? What kind of research was she pursuing? Robin mumbled a few words, then retreated.

Eventually, Bill and Robin got into his car and started the drive back to Boston. He had promised to give her the thousand dollars once they arrived there.

* * *

The drive home started off pleasantly enough. Robin wanted a new nightgown, and Douglas suggested they look for one at a large shopping center in Platts-burgh. He knew the place well. He'd worked right there, in the Grand Union, when he'd been a timo-rous, inhibited high school student. Now he stood be-side the alluring Robin and boldly examined lingerie with her. They fingered the fabrics, considered the colors, and at last he bought her a frivolous little out-fit with brief pink panties.

It was the last happy moment he was ever to spend with her. Back in the car again, she asked him to drive her to Charlestown, Massachusetts, before tak-ing her into Boston. In Charlestown, she went alone to visit a friend, emerging a half hour later with a plastic sandwich bag half full of cocaine. The two of them sampled some of it and then headed for Boston. But the cocaine affected Robin badly. She became anxious and then, suddenly, paranoid. Someone in a yellow Volkswagen was following them, she insisted. A few minutes later, she said someone in a big van was also following them. She couldn't go home, she cried. She'd be followed there. Something dreadful would happen to her. She begged Bill to check her into a motel.

He found one in Natick, the Red Roof Inn, but as soon as he carried in the bags, she said she was sure she'd just seen the yellow Volkswagen go by. They left the motel hurriedly and looked for another, settling at last on one that was set well back from the road. He brought in the bags. She started to unpack. Then, her paranoia suddenly fulminating, she said her pursuers were in the room next door. They checked out of the second motel, too, and looked for still another. While they were driving, taking back roads and deserted streets, she suddenly demanded that he stop the car and hide the cocaine so that she couldn't be caught with it.

Where? How? He pulled over on a quiet residential street and punched the plastic bag into a snowbank in front of one of the houses.

Later that night, ensconced in a third motel, Robin's terrors finally evaporated. But as soon as she felt better, she begged Bill to retrieve the cocaine. It was the middle of the night and freezing cold, but he wanted to assuage her, so he went outside and started the car.

He found the street on which he'd hidden the bag, but he couldn't remember precisely where on the street he'd buried it. Was it ten houses from the corner? Twelve? In the cold dawn he began searching, clambering onto icy lawns and thrusting his hands into snowbanks. His feet grew soaking wet. His fingers numbed. But although he dug and dug, he couldn't find the plastic sandwich bag, and finally, after an hour and a half, he gave up and returned to the motel.

Robin was distraught. The coke had cost her about $700, she said.

In the morning, according to Bill, she told him that she wanted, not just the thousand dollars he had promised her for the night in Plattsburgh, but another $2,000. She said it was because by now she'd been with him not just one day but three.

He said he couldn't afford all that. He said it wasn't his fault that they'd spent all of Friday night trying to get away from whoever she thought was chasing her.

But she stuck to her guns. He owed her $3,000, not just $1,000 or even $2,000.

What had started off for him as a romantic reunion had turned into a nightmare from which he couldn't seem to awaken.

In the next few days, again according to Bill, the two of them were often on the phone with one another, apparently arguing over whether he owed her $2,000 or $3,000. He thought her unreasonable but told himself she'd come around, and on February 22 he made a date with her to discuss the exact amount of his debt.

They met at a roadside restaurant near Lynn, went to a motel, and later were driving around in his car, arguing vociferously, when suddenly Robin sprang on him that he owed her not just $3,000 but $5,000. Her reason: since he hadn't yet paid her a red cent on the initial debt, he owed her $2,000 in interest.

Can Robin have been this usurious? We have only Bill's word that she majestically escalated his financial debt, although several prostitutes who knew her told me they thought it was likely. "Lots of girls do it," one of them said. "You go for what the market will bear." "Robin was that type," said another. "Out and out greedy. Like no matter how many men she'd had in a night, she'd steal your john right from under your nose." A third made the point that Robin might have asked for outrageous interest simply as a way of making Douglas stop pestering her.

Whether or not Robin actually asked Douglas for $2,000 in interest—and, if she did, what her reasons were—is unknowable, but certainly that night something happened to send him into an acute state of alarm. It occurred while he and Robin were driving.

She was talking, he insisted, about the money he owed her. He was disagreeing, bargaining. Suddenly he felt a sharp pain in his chest. All this talk of high interest was more than he could stand. He was having a heart attack, he was sure. Giving up the wheel, he begged her to drive him at once to a hospital.

At the hospital, Lynn Union, he was examined and given an EKG. It showed no heart muscle damage. Nevertheless, the staff thought he didn't seem quite right and, deciding he was having some sort of panic attack, gave him a muscle relaxant. They also advised him not to do any driving while on the medication, and when Robin indicated she wouldn't be taking him home, a nurse telephoned his wife and asked her to come for him.

Bill lay down on a hospital cot. Robin stayed with him. A nurse came in, then left, and as soon as she was gone, Robin started in about the money again. Bill heard her as if through water. He was drowsy, submerging into sleep. Then, suddenly, he felt, or thought he felt, a hideous pain in his ear. He felt, or thought he felt, her driving one of her long-nailed fingers into his ear and he heard, or imagined he heard, her demanding that he pay her what he owed. Dazed, he rolled over onto his other side. She hovered over him and drove her finger into this ear, too. He kept tossing and turning, and no matter which side he rolled onto, she pushed her finger into his ear. At last she let him be, and he slept.

Robin wandered about the hospital room. She looked into the pockets of his brown wool jacket to see if there was any money in it. There wasn't. She opened his briefcase. No money there, either. But it did contain some trays of scientific slides, some grant proposals Bill had been reviewing, and the keys to his car, his house, and the safety deposit box he'd opened at her request. She stuffed the contents of the briefcase into her large handbag. Inside, she saw that she still had the little pink panties from the nightgown set he'd bought her in Plattsburgh. She pulled them out and, as if in exchange for what she had taken, tucked them into the pocket of his jacket.

She almost left after that, but in the end she decided to linger for a while. Nancy was coming. Perhaps she relished the thought of how shocked the suburban housewife would be to see her there by her sick husband. Patiently, she sat at Bill's bedside and waited.

Nancy, concerned and confused, arrived at the hospital accompanied by a neighbor she'd asked to drive her to Lynn. The two women entered Bill's room. They saw him lying pale and prostrate. And they saw at his side a pretty postadolescent girl.

"I'm Chris," the girl said boldly. Then she hurried out of the hospital and disappeared.

"That's the girl, isn't it?" Nancy whispered, but the neighbor overheard.

Bill acknowledged that it was.

Nancy, humiliated, was silent on the way home.

The keys to the safety deposit box were of immediate interest to Robin. In the days when Bill had been flush with Tufts research funds, he'd often stashed away money in the box, so bright and early the next morning she went to the First National Bank in Boston and, keys in hand, requested box number 920. An attendant checked the records, determined that the box was registered in the names of both Robin Benedict and William Douglas, and allowed her to unlock it.

The box was empty. She left the vault precipitously and, apparently suspecting now that if Bill had any money he must be keeping it at home, asked the attendant if she might use the telephone. She called Bill and told him she was coming out to his house.

He went into a panic. Robin in Sharon! Robin at his *home*. He was no longer as eager to see her as he had been only a week earlier. The sensation of having long-nailed fingers driven into his ears the night before was still sharp within him. She might try to hurt him again. Worse, how could he be sure she was coming alone? Maybe she was bringing her pimp. Or some other of her associates. Once, long before, she'd told him how she'd gotten friends of hers to beat up a cab driver who'd insulted her. Who knew what she might do to him? Frightened, he telephoned the Sharon Police Department.

A sergeant answered, and Douglas told him that the night before he'd been with a woman and she'd stolen his briefcase. Now she'd telephoned and said she was coming to his home to extort money from him in exchange for the briefcase.

The sergeant assigned a police officer to go over to Douglas's house.

Douglas was inside the conventional clapboard ranch house, explaining the situation to police officer James Testa, when Robin's silver Toyota pulled up in the driveway. She was alone, he saw at once, and all of a sudden he felt ridiculous for having called the police. What if she discovered he'd done that? What would she think of him? He raced outdoors and, cornering her as she began crossing his lawn, begged her to talk with him in the driveway.

It was useless. She wanted to go inside to look for

the money. The two of them began shouting at each other, and soon they were making such a commotion that Officer Testa hurried out of the house to keep them from disturbing the Sharon peace. The sight of the cop enraged Robin even further, just as Douglas had anticipated. She began screaming that he had stolen something from *her*. "Give me back what belongs to me," she yelled, "and I will give you back what belongs to you."

Officer Testa made them both come down to the station house and, thinking they were having a mere lovers' quarrel, gave them a lecture. They should try to work out their problem in a more mature fashion, he told them.

During the next few days, Robin's life was filled with activities that had nothing to do with Douglas. One afternoon, she sought out a friend from her high school days who had become a carpenter and took him to see the renovations in her new house. She wanted his opinion on whether the work was being done right. Another day, she went home to Methuen to attend the funeral of an aunt. Afterward, she paid a call on another high school friend, and over coffee told him, too, about the ambitious renovations, even about the handsome curtains she had just bought. Like Zola's Nana, who before her untimely demise was preoccupied with redesigning her bedroom, Robin struck her friends as having nothing on her mind but interior decoration. But in fact she was still locked into her financial dispute with Douglas, and she continued to do battle with him on the telephone. One time she told him that if he didn't pay up, she'd go to the Boston newspapers with the story of their relationship. Then she threatened to come to his house again. And one day, about a week after her first visit, she made good on the threat. She drove to Sharon and, telephoning from the firehouse in town, shouted so loudly that a fireman overheard her say, "I have your slides and the other items. I am going to come over now."

Bill dissuaded her. He promised her that if only she would leave Sharon, he would meet her somewhere else and, in exchange for his possessions, pay her. So, on March 2, they met on a busy Boston street corner.

He went to the assignation with $1,000 in cash in his pocket. Flat broke, he'd gotten the money from Nancy, who—allegedly without asking any questions about why he needed it—had borrowed $2,000 from her father. He'd put half the loan into his microscope case in a bedroom closet and pocketed the other half, thinking that possibly he could get Robin to settle— despite her increasing demands—for just one grand.

He failed. She asserted more adamantly than ever that he still owed her $5,000—$3,000 for the trip to Plattsburgh and $2,000 in interest. He wrote out a check for $200—her fee for meeting with him—and, keeping the wad of cash in his pocket, didn't even try to placate her with the thousand he'd brought along.

Perhaps he had decided it would be useless. Or perhaps he had by now gotten the faintest glimmer of a solution to his predicament. Perhaps the notion of killing her had at last begun begging and beating at his brain. After all, some tide in their relationship had turned. Now it was no longer he who was hounding her for visits, but she who was hounding him. And he was no longer writing her letters. The days when he had opened up shyly to her and extolled her for being "You You You You You" were long behind him, banished finally and forever by her outrageous demands

ever since the trip to Plattsburgh and by the vicious
cruelty she had displayed the night of his panic attack. Indeed, he no longer felt that he loved her. The
passion he had always secretly longed to have
stopped had, at last, come to an end.

Robin had dinner with her parents that day. She
acted carefree, joking with her father, trying on
clothes with her sister. She told the family that she
and J.R. would be getting their wallpaper on Sunday,
and that as soon as everything was finished, she'd
have them over to *her* house for a meal. She knew her
father was uneasy about her living with a black man,
she said, but if he got to know J.R., he might feel
differently about the matter.

She also mentioned Professor Douglas. Her parents had met him in court on one of the occasions
when she'd been arrested, and they'd chosen to believe him when he said he was her employer. They
hadn't liked him, but they'd been impressed. Well,
lately, said Robin, the man had become a pest. He'd
been following her, bothering her. That very day
she'd gotten so mad that she'd telephoned his wife at
her job and told her to tell her husband to lay off.

The call to Nancy must have seemed to Douglas like
a kind of final straw, for two days afterward, on March
4, he notified his bank to stop payment on the $200
check. It was Friday afternoon. Given what he knew
of Robin, he would have been certain that when the
banks opened on Monday and she discovered his per-
fidy, she would be violently angry. So it seems likely
that he meant for her never to find out, that he had
decided, that Friday afternoon, to do away with her
over the weekend. Of course, it will never be possible

to say with absolute certainty that he ever actually *decided* to do away with her. When he confessed to having killed her, he said he'd done so accidentally, and he denied having set a trap for her and luring her into it. Yet his first move, as soon as he'd stopped the check, was to telephone Robin and tell her that he'd pay her, and pay her in cash, if she would meet him one last time and hand over to him his possessions. His second was to suggest that their meeting take place in Sharon.

This was surprising, given his earlier resistance to having Robin visit him there. Suddenly, he did an about-face, and instead of being dismayed and frightened at her coming to his home, he began urging her to do so. Indeed, if she would come to the house, he told her, he would pay her *all* she said he owed. He informed her of this over the telephone on the evening he stopped payment on the check, and he repeated it to her again the next morning.

The second time he proposed it, Robin agreed to the suggestion. She'd be at his home later that night, she said. She wasn't sure just when, but she'd call and let him know.

Apparently, it didn't cross her mind that this might be a dangerous visit. Apparently, she didn't sense that she had been goading Bill beyond his endurance. Yet, why not? Her parents didn't trust him. The day they met him, he'd given Shirley Benedict the creeps by boasting that he knew everything there was to know about chemistry, even how to concoct poisons that could kill a person and yet go undetected in the body. Nor did J.R. trust him. And on the day she made her final date with the professor, her street-smart boyfriend questioned the wisdom of her going to his house alone.

Robin ignored her lover's concern. Her attitude seemed to be that she knew perfectly well how to take care of herself, and just as she had defied her parents in regard to living with Costic and J.R., she defied J.R.'s anxieties about Douglas. She and the professor had reached an understanding, she declared; he'd definitely be paying up tonight, and she'd go there alone, thank you.

Perhaps she was, as Detective Dwyer had said, a girl bent on rebellion. Or perhaps, with the lack of self-regard that Dwyer's boss had noticed in her the day he'd predicted she'd end up in the river, she was courting, had all along been courting, her own destruction.

Whatever her reasons, Robin made her date with Douglas and then went nonchalantly about her business that Saturday afternoon. In the early hours, she shopped for a birthday present for Taj, Savi and J.R.'s son, who was going to be celebrating his fourth birthday the next day. Later, she dressed carefully for work, laying out her jewelry and clothes on the brass bed at the house in Malden before putting them on— gold earrings and a gold knot ring, brown pants, a beige shirt, and an expensive beige corduroy jacket she'd bought at Lord & Taylor's.

In the late afternoon she left the house and went out to her car, and it is possible that for a brief moment, just before she got behind the wheel, she experienced a sudden change of mind about visiting Douglas, or at least an urge to discuss the matter further with J.R. A neighbor saw her acting uncharacteristically indecisive. She approached her car, then walked away from it, then returned and stood beside it for a long time, all the while staring wistfully back at the house. But, after this, Robin unlocked the door with her usual devil-may-care swiftness, and hurriedly drove off.

She drove into Boston and started hooking. She'd rented a new trick pad, this one on elegant Beacon Street again, and she went over there for a while and used some cocaine, scraping up the powdry white lines with a new hobby knife. Then she went to Good Time Charlie's and hung out at the bar for a bit. From time to time she called Douglas and said she'd be leaving for Sharon soon, but she was busy just now and would call him again when she knew what time she'd be starting out. At about 9 P.M. she went on a date to meet an aristocratic new john. He came from one of the oldest families in Boston and lived in one of the city's newest, most fashionable buildings. He'd heard about Robin from the building's doorman, who'd met her a few weeks before at the bar of the Park Plaza Hotel and arranged the date for him.

Robin's new john, whose business was real estate, let her into his apartment, got her a drink, and chatted with her for about twenty-five minutes. She told him about how she'd attended the Rhode Island School of Design and how she was working as a prostitute just temporarily, just until she got together enough money to invest in something and retire. She thought it might take her three or four years.

He was very much taken with her. He is the kind of man, he likes to boast, who never misses a detail because if he does, he "loses a million." Robin's details impressed him mightily. She spoke well and was well dressed. He felt he could have taken her anywhere on a date, "even to the Harvard Club."

After a while he asked her to spend the night. But she said that tonight she was available only for "something quick." She couldn't stay because there was something else she had to do. He didn't want a quickie, so he gave her $30 for the time she'd spent talking to him, and they agreed they'd get together some other night. Then she asked to use his phone, and she dialed a number. He overheard her saying, "I'll be leaving shortly. I'll be there in about a half hour."

When she hung up, she said to the new john, by way of explanation, "I have to run in and out between the wife and children."

Douglas's evening was far more tense. He'd made arrangements to have Nancy and the children out of the house by telling his wife that Robin was coming and that he intended to settle up and be done with her. Nancy had agreed that under the circumstances, it would be best if the family were gone, so she'd taken the boys out and sent Pammy baby-sitting. But Robin was taking forever about getting to Sharon, and he began to worry that she might not arrive before Nancy and the kids returned. Because he was so edgy—or so he said—he began telephoning Robin's answering service and, impersonating J.R., picking up her messages. Then, at last, she called at about 9:30 P.M. and said she was on her way. He waited a little while and then once again dialed her answering service, this time leaving a message *for* Robin. The message purported to be from a man named Joe who lived in Charlestown, and it was that there was going to be an all-night party at his place, commencing at 10:30 P.M. that night and lasting until 6 P.M. on Sunday, and that Robin was invited.

Why did he leave that message? the Norfolk County D.A.'s office was to demand of Douglas when he finally confessed. Why, because Robin had been teasing him all night about coming to Sharon and hadn't shown up, he said. And so, "when she didn't come at ten o'clock, I decided that since she was stringing me along, I would tease her... and send her on a wild goose chase to Charlestown. She would waste time and waste money, and time was money to her."

Maybe that was why he made the call. But maybe not. Certainly it was a call that—at least for a time—got him right off the hook, threw suspicion for the events that subsequently transpired away from him and onto the unsuspecting Joe in Charlestown.

Those events, grizzly and gruesome, would soon begin racing to their conclusion. I learned about them from Douglas's confession, a lengthly, rambling account that took him two days to make. But they can be rapidly reported, swiftly recounted. They were hideous.

Robin pulled up at the house in Sharon at about 10:45 P.M. Bill let her in, saying, "Come in quickly and shut the door," and she immediately demanded, "Do you have the money?"

He told her he did, but that he didn't want to give it to her downstairs. There were too many windows; the neighbors might see him with a woman not his wife. He asked her to come upstairs. That's where the money was, anyway, he told her. He'd put it in a drawer in the microscope case he kept in his bedroom closet.

She led the way, and they went upstairs and into the bedroom. He opened the closet, bending down toward the microscope case and pulling open a little drawer. He extricated the money—hundred-dollar bills, all folded small and rolled together. He started to stand up. Then, as he straightened up, he told her that $2,000 was all she would be getting because it was all he had. He reached out to hand it to her. And then—or so he said—she hit him over the head with a hammer.

She had brought it with her, he claimed, and concealed it under her jacket. He hadn't noticed it, he insisted, although it was a two-and-a-half-pound sledgehammer. She hit him with it several times, striking him on his head, legs, arms, and trunk. He fell backward onto his bed, a king-size bed on which he and Nancy and the kids used to curl up to watch TV, and she loomed over him. Suddenly he lunged upward, twisted her wrist with one hand, grabbed the hammer with the other, and began pushing *her* down onto the bed.

She started screaming. She shrieked that he was a bum and that he owed her $5,000, not just $2,000. She hit him and kicked him and sunk her teeth into the inside of his thigh. He lifted the hammer and brought it crashing down on her skull.

The hammer touched flesh, and it seemed to him to keep right on going. It cracked her skull, and he could see not just skin but brain tissue. He hit her again. And then maybe a third time. He couldn't be sure how many blows he struck, but by the end of the second or third time he hit her, the hammer had penetrated her skull an inch and a half.

He was dazed, crazed, beside himself. But a few seconds later he came to his senses. He leaned over her and tried to take her pulse. But he felt nothing, neither on the inside of her wrist nor at the carotid artery on her neck, and he knew that he had killed her. "My God!" was the first thought that flashed through his mind. "My God! What if Billy and Pammy and John walked in through that door?"

It was a horrible thought, more horrible to him than what he had done, and it mobilized him, made him leap into activity so that his brutality might never be known to them.

He attended, first, to himself. His head wound was bleeding copiously, so he went into the bathroom and, scooping up some towels, pressed them firmly against his forehead, attempting to staunch the blood. It worked, and as soon as the bleeding subsided, he lowered his trousers and checked the inside of his thigh, where Robin had bitten him. He could see her teethmarks on his flesh, but fortunately the bite hadn't pierced the surface of his skin.

He was ready, then, for housekeeping. Pulling up his trousers and clutching the bloodstained towels, he ran to the hall closet, where Nancy kept a stack of old paper shopping bags. He grabbed one and returned to the bedroom. Robin's jacket was covered with blood, and so was the old blue shirt he himself was wearing, so he removed his shirt and shoved it and the jacket into the shopping bag. Then he tried to hide the weapon. But where? Momentarily disoriented, he grabbed a blue windbreaker from the back of the closet and tried to conceal the hammer in one of its capacious pockets. But the pocket was far too small. Hanging the jacket back in the closet, he threw the hammer into the brown bag. Then he noticed that blood was starting to seep through the bag. If he wasn't careful, the weight of the hammer would rip it right open. He ran into the kitchen, got a plastic garbage bag this time, and dumped the contents of the brown bag into that.

There was blood all over. Blood on the comforter on which Robin lay dead. Blood on the floor. Blood on the radiator behind the bed. It wasn't a lot of blood, but it was splattered here and there throughout the room. Most of it was his own, from the wounds Robin had inflicted on him. She seemed hardly to be bleeding at all. Still, it was important that there be no blood in the house at all, none, not even his own. He ran back to the bathroom, grabbed the hand towels he had used to clean himself, and began wiping up the gore with them and stuffing them into the brown paper bag. Then he got dressed, putting on a warm ski jacket with huge, deep pockets and somehow managing to cram the brown bag full of towels into one of the pockets. Finally, he went over to the bed and, with Robin still lying in the middle of the comforter, began to pull the comforter and the blankets beneath it off the bed. He made a kind of cradle that way and, holding the four ends, rocked Robin's body down the stairs and into the kitchen.

Now he was ready to leave. He would take her car, he decided. That way there would be no trace of her having been to his house. He went out to her car, but when he got inside, he couldn't start it. The keys weren't in the ignition, where she usually left them.

Back in the house, he began searching for them. Where had she put them? He looked in her pocketbook, but they weren't there. He thrust his hands deep inside the dead girl's pants pockets, but they weren't there either. At last he forced himself to open the plastic bag and rummage through the pockets of her bloody corduroy jacket. He found the keys.

Going outside, he backed the car up to the deck, which was adjacent to the kitchen, and returning inside, dragged the body, still swaddled in the quilt, out of doors. The Christmas tree he and Nancy had gotten for the children in December had been discarded out on the deck, and the planks were slippery with pine needles. He pulled the comforter through the needles and hefted it into the hatchback.

The town was silent, its crescents and side streets dark. He drove for a while, taking back roads, then realized he didn't really know how to get rid of Robin, how to get rid of her remains. He pulled over and sat motionless, worrying the problem over and over in his head. And just then—or so he was to say—he remembered the call he had made to her answering service, the call about the party at Joe's in Charlestown. If he telephoned the answering service now and left a message *from* Robin for J.R., one that indicated she'd gone to the party, it would give him time. J.R. would believe that Robin was in Charlestown, at the allnight celebration, and wouldn't worry about her. The thought spurred him on and he started the car, drove to a nearby shopping mall, and placed the call. The voice in which he spoke to the answering service was pitched high and sultry, a girl's voice.

After that, still with no clear idea of what he was going to do, he started driving south on I-95. But as he drove, he kept thinking that some of Robin's associates might have known she was going to his house. Suppose they came looking for her? Suppose they were already there? Nervous, he stopped the car at a rest area on the road and telephoned Nancy. "Is there anyone there?" he demanded. "Were there any calls?"

Nancy said she'd just walked in the door and asked where he was. He didn't tell her. He just said, "I have a problem and I'll tell you about it later," then hung up abruptly. But moments later he realized he'd forgotten to instruct her to lock all the doors. He called her back and directed her to do so. He used his credit card to make both those calls.

Then, standing there after he'd hung up again, he noticed that the rest area was replete with garbage barrels and dumpsters. Maybe he could get rid of the plastic bag with the bloodied clothes and hammer in one of them. It was a great idea, he thought. But there were several cars and tractor-trailers parked at the rest area. Some of them had their lights on. Most likely the drivers weren't sleeping. They might notice him. Frustrated, he got back into the car and, making a U-turn, began driving north.

In a few minutes, a sign for another rest area appeared. He pulled over. This rest stop was deserted. Moving quickly, he opened the Toyota's hatch, removed the plastic bag, and heaved it into a trash barrel.

Back in the car and continuing north, he thought briefly, and for the first time since he had killed Robin, that perhaps he ought to confess. After all, the killing hadn't been entirely unprovoked. After all, she'd been trying to extort money from him. And she'd hit *him* with the hammer. He had deep wounds to prove it. The police might feel some sympathy for him. Detective Dwyer might. He decided that he would drive into Boston and turn Robin's body and himself over to Dwyer. But when he reached the city, he knew he couldn't do it. No one would understand. So he just kept driving. After a while he came to a gas station and filled up the tank of the Toyota. He credited the purchase to his own registration number, not Robin's.

* * *

Later, passing the Boston train station, he got out and telephoned Nancy again, once more demanding to know if anyone had been to the house and whether she and the kids were all right. Nancy wanted to know what was going on, but he wouldn't tell her.

He drove some more. He drove right through the Combat Zone, where he had first met Robin, and along Commonwealth Avenue, where he had once broken into her apartment. Eventually he came to Brookline, and there, on a quiet residential street, he saw a garbage dumpster and decided to put her body into it.

His mind made up, he got out of the car went around to the back, and started to haul her out. Suddenly, he jumped. The body was making a noise. It was not a breath but a sort of eerie sound, the sound of the residual air in her lungs being expelled. It was a sound he would never forget.

Nor would he ever forget, he said, the way, at precisely the same moment, a light came on in a house close to where he was standing. Petrified, he banged down the door of the hatchback and, keeping Robin's body inside, got back in the car and started driving again.

He drove for hours. At one point during the night he found himself in Pawtucket, Rhode Island, and stopped for a cup of coffee at a Howard Johnson's. Then he made his way from Pawtucket to Providence. There, he left the highway and came to a large housing complex and shopping center. He saw a big supermarket, a Radio Shack, a Rhode Island blood bank, and lots of dumpsters. The sun was starting to come up. It was now or never. He got out of the car and, removing several bags of garbage from a loaded dumpster, made room for his own discards. Then, seizing the bloody comforter, blankets, and Robin's body, he shoved them into the trash. He was done with her now.

That morning, Nancy met him at the bus station near their home in Sharon. He'd telephoned her from Providence, where he'd parked Robin's car in a lot after throwing her pocketbook and the bloody towels in various dumpsters, and asked her to pick him up. But although she complied, she was in a stormy mood. She kept insisting that he tell her what was going on.

He said he didn't want to talk about it.

She said, "I've got a right to know. You were out all night."

He started to make up a lie, started to pretend he'd been in Boston all night, and then, without meaning to, broke down and spilled out what had happened. They were on the road, nearly home, early church-goers passing them on the quiet Sunday morning streets, and he blurted out that he'd killed the girl.

Nancy responded as any wife might. She began screaming. But he was bewildered. He'd always thought of her as a quiet, controlled person, and now here she was, positively hysterical, and one of the things she was yelling and screaming about was that he shouldn't have told her. This, even though she'd pushed him to it. Resentful, but hoping to calm her down, he swore to her that no matter what happened in the future, he would never ever admit to anyone that he'd told her of the killing. Then, together, they entered their home.

* * *

Inside, he went into the bedroom, shut the door, and checked his head wound. He'd been wearing a tight knitted cap over it, but as soon as he removed the cap, the wound opened up and started bleeding. He sopped up the blood with tissues, flushed them away, and made himself a proper bandage. Then he went out, drove to a grocery store in a nearby town, and called Robin's answering service. Once again using his girl's falsetto, he pretended to be Robin herself, with a message for J.R. She'd left Joe's in Charlestown, ran the message, and was going over now to visit that rich new john she'd been with the evening before. His voice high, he trilled out the address. He'd jotted it down the night before while monitoring her calls.

Back in his bedroom at home, he made his final plans. So far, everything had gone nearly perfectly. He'd really gotten things under control. But there was still the matter of Robin's car. He'd have to get rid of it. But how? He thought about the scientific meeting he was supposed to attend in Washington the next day. Perhaps he could go back to Providence, get Robin's car, and dispose of it in Washington. Or, better yet, dispose of it on the *way* to Washington. He decided that was the best idea. He'd get Nancy to drive him back to the bus station. He'd tell her, since she'd said she wanted to know nothing further about the killing, that he was taking the bus into Boston in order to catch his train to Washington. But, in fact, he'd take a bus to Providence, get the car, abandon it somewhere safe, and *then* catch a train to Washington.

In the meantime, before he had to leave, he'd best dispose of the contents of Robin's pocketbook. Getting

out a scissors, he cut her driver's license into tiny
pieces; later he would toss away the pieces. But he
couldn't bear to part with her new little address book.
It made him so curious. He kept it, hiding it in his
bedroom alongside the pink panties she'd tucked in
his pocket the night of his false-alarm heart attack.

Savi Bisram called Douglas a couple of times that afternoon. Robin hadn't shown up for Taj's birthday
party, and since it was altogether unlike her to disap-
point the child, she was afraid something might have
happened to her. Had he seen her?

Not since midnight, he said, since Savi seemed to
know that they'd had an appointment. Robin hadn't
stayed long, he went on. They'd talked, looked at
some porno slides, and then around midnight she'd
gone off to some party. In Charlestown, he thought.
Then he told Savi he was sorry he couldn't be of more
help, but he was leaving town shortly to attend a conference in Washington. Later, he must have feared
he'd sounded callous, for he called her back and, not
reaching her, left a message for her with another
hooker friend. If Savi needed any more assistance
from him, he said, she could reach him at his Washington hotel. He left the number.

Late in the day, he proceeded with his plan to get rid
of Robin's car. Nancy drove him to the bus station; he
was, had anyone noticed him that chilly Sunday afternoon, just another suburban husband being
chauffeured by his wife, hurrying to catch a commuter bus to Boston, waving a fond goodbye. But as
soon as Nancy drove off he went not to Boston but to
Providence. He took Robin's car out of the Providence
lot and drove it to New York. He parked it in a garage

close to the railroad station and, removing the inspection sticker and license plates, abandoned it. Feeling more secure than he had in hours, he then walked from the garage to New York's Pennsylvania Station and bought a train ticket to Washington.

He arrived in Washington at around 8 A.M. on Monday, March 7, and it must have seemed to him, at that moment, that he had committed the perfect crime, engineered the perfect cover-up. He had disposed of both the body and the car, and he had planted clues, all sorts of clues, suggesting that Robin had been with other people after she left him—and therefore she had obviously been alive when she left his house. If his luck continued to hold, the car would never even be discovered. It would sit in the garage for years. If his luck continued to hold, Robin's body would never be found. It would be crushed by a garbage compactor and incinerated or buried. And if he was *really* lucky, people would assume that the always erratic, always unpredictable Robin had just decided to leave town.

Did he never for a moment that weekend think of how he had once loved her? I remember expecting, as I leafed through his confession, that sometime soon he would refer to his long-gone passion, express, if not remorse, at least nostalgia. But in fact whenever he spoke of Robin, he did so with, at best, disdain, at worst, something far stranger, more impersonal.

Ultimately, it was as a result of one of these impersonal references to Robin that I grasped the emotional distance he had at last achieved from her. Describing to the district attorney's staff how he had hoisted her body into the dumpster, he referred to it as "the material." It was so strikingly peculiar and inappropriate a word that even the detective who was interrogating him—Lieutenant James Sharkey, a man with over thirty years on the Massachusetts State Police force—was brought up short. "'Material' being the body?" he interrupted Douglas. And Douglas said yes, he'd meant Robin's body, although of course it was wrapped in the comforter at the time, so he'd lumped the two together in his phrase.

Shadows

One day, long after Douglas had been caught and sentenced for the murder of Robin Benedict, Lieutenant Sharkey commented to me, "Our catching the professor was really just a matter of coincidence. He almost went scot-free. But there was one thing he didn't consider. About a month before he did away with Robin, Massachusetts went ecological and passed a bottle law. It was the bottle law that put Douglas behind bars."

Sharkey was joking with me. He's a garrulous, wisecracking Irish cop, who never answers a "How are you?" without a "Couldn't be better if I was twins" or "Ready to run off with ya, but don't tell your husband." In fact, he and his staff worked heroically to put Douglas behind bars, and the police work that went into solving the case was meticulous. But there was some truth to his observation, for if it wasn't for the bottle law, the police at the Norfolk County D.A.'s office might never have had the opportunity to do their work because the fact that Robin had been murdered might never have emerged.

The bottle law is the law that enables anyone returning beer or soda cans or bottles to obtain a refund. When it first went into effect in Massachusetts, middle-class, relatively comfortable people hardly gave it a thought. But those who were out of work or otherwise economically strapped immediately saw the law as a bonanza, a way to make a bit of cash by scavenging for cans and bottles.

Thus it was that on Sunday, March 6, two unemployed men, Joseph Plotegher and Robert Jewell, both of them with families to support, decided to go out scavenging on I-95. It was a cold morning, but they pursued their task assiduously, checking for cans on the side of the highway and, in particular, in the trash barrels at rest stops. At a rest stop near Foxboro, Plotegher peered into one trash barrel and saw a large brown plastic bag, knotted at the top. He hefted it out and, curious because it was unusually heavy, ripped it open. Inside were a beige jacket, a blue shirt, and a small sledgehammer, all covered with blood.

Plotegher was frightened. He called Jewell over to look at the items, and the friends conferred. It was clear that the things were ghastly. But should they report them? If they did, mightn't they be accused of some kind of foul play? Nervous, the two men decided to put the plastic bag back into the trash barrel, leave the rest area, and continue their search elsewhere. But after a couple of hours Plotegher's conscience started to bother him. Suppose some dangerous criminal was on the loose? Determined to do what was right, he went home and telephoned the State Police at Foxboro to report what he'd seen.

A young state trooper named Paul Landry was the first of many policemen who would eventually become involved in the case. On Sunday afternoon he went to the rest area, examined the bloody jacket, shirt, and sledgehammer, had them photographed by another trooper, and took them back to the Foxboro barracks, where he logged them into the contraband journal. On Monday morning, at precisely the time Douglas reached Washington, Landry turned the materials over to a police chemist for analysis. Working on the assumption that he might be able to connect the property to someone who'd disappeared, he spent the remainder of Monday checking police teletypes about recently reported missing persons.

Landry didn't learn anything useful from the teletyped reports, but the following day, Tuesday, March 8, a fellow police officer mentioned that he'd heard a story about a missing girl on a television news program the previous night. He didn't recall what channel. Landry contacted all the local channels, to no avail; but late in the afternoon, one of the channels called back and said yes, they'd aired a brief report about a missing girl the evening before. She was from Malden.

A few minutes later, Landry was on the phone to the Malden Police Department. Sure enough, a Clarence J. Rogers had reported that his live-in girlfriend, Robin Benedict, had been missing since Sunday, March 6. The police sergeant over in Malden said that according to information he'd gathered, Rogers might be a pimp and Benedict might be a prostitute. He also said that apparently the girl had last been known to be going to Sharon to pay a call on a William H. J. Douglas, Ph.D.

What had she been wearing when she disappeared? Landry asked the Malden police sergeant. Slacks, a beige shirt, and a beige jacket, he was told.

Landry reported back to his supervisors that he had an ID on the person who had, in all likelihood, owned the beige jacket. On an official level, the Benedict case had begun.

It had already begun on an unofficial level. By Tuesday the eighth, J.R. had hired a private detective agency to help him search for Robin. He felt certain that whatever had happened to her, William Douglas had had something to do with it. And even as Trooper Landry was talking with the Malden police sergeant, Jack Da Rosa and Jim Smith of Boston's Central Secret Service Bureau were en route to Washington, D.C., to scout out Douglas.

Da Rosa and Smith knew where he was staying because he'd left his phone number for Savi Bisram. They checked into his hotel, the Hotel Washington on Pennsylvania Avenue, and by 10:30 P.M., they had persuaded Douglas to let them come to his room. They were investigating the case of a missing girl, they told him, and they understood he knew her.

Sure, he knew her, he said. She was a prostitute who worked out of Good Time Charlie's. Sure, their information was right; sure, she'd been to see him at his home on Saturday night. But she'd left at about midnight to go to a party. Had the detectives looked into the whereabouts of some contact of hers in Charlestown, a guy named Joe?

The private eyes listened impassively. Then one of

them, noticing that Douglas was wearing a large, three-by-three-inch bandage on his forehead, asked him what was wrong. He said he'd walked smack into a kitchen cabinet at home just before he'd come down to Washington.

When was that? Da Rosa and Smith also asked him. He'd taken a train down from Massachusetts on Monday, March 7, he said.

Why hadn't he flown down? they wanted to know. Because, he explained, he'd had a lot of paperwork to do in connection with the meeting—an important meeting of the Veterans' Administration Merit Board—and taking the train had given him a perfect opportunity to get the work done.

Soon the two detectives left, but they paid Douglas a second visit about an hour later, and this time, when the subject of his head wound came up, he told them that it had happened as the result of a mugging. Someone had tried to steal his briefcase and in the scuffle had hit him over the head with it. The incident had occured in Washington's train station, he said.

Contradictory and nervous, he struck Da Rosa and Smith as suspicious, and they asked him if they could take a look around. He must have been afraid that to refuse would somehow be incriminating, for he said okay. Then, trembling, he stood by warily while they searched the room cursorily. In his suitcase, tucked between his clothes, were the license plates he had removed from Robin's Toyota. But although Da Rosa and Smith opened the suitcase, they didn't discover the plates, and the next day they headed back to Boston, leaving him to finish his conference.

* * *

Back in New England, the private eyes were informed by the Malden police that the police over in Foxboro had in their possession a jacket that might have belonged to Robin. And on Monday, March 14, they and their client, J.R., as well as Robin Benedict's father, were taken to the State Police Chemical Lab in Boston to view the jacket and see if they could identify it.

Trooper Landry and the chemist who had analyzed the bloodstains produced the beige corduroy jacket and showed it to J.R. and Benedict separately. J.R. was first. The chemist raised the jacket. Suddenly J.R. became visibly upset and began to shout "No, no! That's hers! No! No!"

His reaction, so extreme and so volatile, made Landry suspicious, and he grabbed the jacket and took it closer, placing it right under J.R.'s nose and demanding that he smell it. The jacket, everyone who handled it had observed, still bore a strong odor of perfume despite the dried blood on it. Did J.R. recognize the smell? Landry asked. But J.R., violently upset now, took one sniff at the jacket and started to run out of the room. Landry got him back; then, somewhat subdued, J.R. stated that without a doubt, the perfume was the kind his girlfriend, Robin Benedict, used to wear. He was certain of it because he'd bought her the scent.

A few minutes later, Landry showed the jacket to John Benedict, who said it was definitely his daughter's. She'd worn it on a visit home only the week before, and he remembered it distinctly because there'd been some talk about it. His other daughter, Rhonda, had coveted it, and she'd tried it on, admired the fit, and half grudgingly given it back, joking that

Robin could keep it because Rhonda didn't like the style of the collar. As John Benedict described the conversation, tears welled up in his eyes.

Right after the incident in the lab, Landry believed that J.R., who had seemed to be overreacting, had killed Robin. But during the week that followed he changed his mind. He spent that week learning everything he could about Robin Benedict and her movements just prior to her disappearance. He spoke to Savi Bisram and some of Robin's other hooker friends. He visited her trick pads, talked to the operators at her answering service, interviewed the real estate man she'd been with before going to Douglas's house, and tracked down the mysterious Joe from Charlestown. And he heard about William Douglas's obsession with Robin, about the Tufts investigation, and about how the professor had haunted the young prostitute at the Saugus health club and quarreled violently with her in front of Officer Testa of the Sharon police. At last, on March 19, almost two weeks after the murder, Landry called Douglas down to the Foxboro police barracks.

It was an unsettling interview. Douglas stuck to his story that although he'd known Robin, he knew nothing about her disappearance. Yet, throughout the interview, there was something peculiar about the scholar's demeanor, something untrustworthy about his responses. Landry couldn't quite put his finger on it. But in any event the shirt that had been found in the barrel was a man's size 17–34, a size that would fit the thick-necked Douglas. And the shirt, as well as the hammer and Robin's jacket, had been located a mere five miles from Douglas's house—the last place Robin was known to have been going. Given these facts, Landry reported to his supervisors after his interview with Douglas that there was probable cause to believe that Robin Benedict had not just disappeared, but had been murdered, and probable cause to believe that William Douglas might have been responsible.

That night the case was turned over to a judge, and several state troopers, under the supervision of Lieutenant Sharkey, obtained a search warrant and proceeded to search Douglas's house.

Lieutenant Sharkey was christened James Henry Horace Michael Patrick Francis Sharkey. "I was named for all my six uncles, and only one of them left me any money," he likes to joke. A tough-minded detective who has helped to solve many of Norfolk County's most baffling crimes, he is rugged-looking, with the face of a character actor who even when young could never play romantic leads.

Sharkey was to get to know William Douglas better, perhaps, than anyone else had ever known the secretive professor. He interviewed him repeatedly, read his private files and correspondence, examined his stockpile of pornography, tailed after him to all manner of assignations, and eventually heard his intimate confession. Knowing Douglas so well gave Sharkey a kind of attachment to the man. He would always maintain—even though he would be mocked for it by those of his colleagues who saw Douglas as a malevolent, unnatural genius—that the professor was likable. He would always maintain that the man had been no match for Robin and that, in fact, few men were a match for today's new breed of prostitutes. Even himself. "When I got into this case, I thought I knew everything," he told me. "But it's a new world out there in the Combat Zone. I've seen girls there who frighten even me." And he would always maintain that he felt sorry for the professor.

He certainly felt sorry for the Douglas family. By the night of the search, the emotional chaos that had overtaken the lives of the Douglases had assumed a virtually palpable existence in the house. The rooms were filthy, utterly disordered. There were stacks of dirty dishes in the kitchen sink. There was decaying food on every counter. In the laundry, the washer had long before overflowed, and the floor was covered with greasy, soapy water. In the master bedroom, there were piles and piles of newspapers, with cockroaches crawling in them. Sharkey told me that it was as if Nancy had gone on strike and Douglas into a remote world of his own. "What got me," he said, "what would always be some sort of a symbol for me, was that downstairs in the family room there was a bulletin board, and on it a note written in a child's handwriting. It said, 'Won't somebody please clean up this house?'"

But if Sharkey felt sorry for the family, it didn't affect the quality of his detective work. He was full of wiles. "Douglas was arrogant that night," he told me, explaining what had happened. "He was looking down his nose at me. So when I read him his rights and wrote down his statements, I just played along with him. I took down his words, but every once in a while I'd stop and ask him how you spelled something, letting him think I was as stupid as he thought I was. It worked like a charm. I think he felt he could say anything he liked around me, and I just wouldn't get it."

With Nancy he was equally cunning but softer. Indeed, his cunning lay in his gentleness with her. She

had been extremely shaken when the police arrived
—at about 12:30 A.M.—and Sharkey had consoled
her and even held her hand. When she asked him if
she could take the children out to a neighbor's, he
said what a good idea that was and that she could if
she wanted to. She didn't, but by then he had won
her confidence, and, as a result, he was shortly able
to obtain from her a bit of evidence that was ultimately to prove extremely damning to Douglas. The
evidence was a bit of thread.

Sharkey and his men had brought with them the
blue shirt that had been found in the trash barrel. It
had been mended under the armpits, and Sharkey
commented on the mending and showed it to Nancy.
Had she sewn it? he asked, and if so, would she mind
showing him the thread she'd used? Nancy said she
thought it looked like her sewing, and she went to the
bureau drawer and got out a spool of thread. Sharkey
contemplated it thoughtfully, then asked her if she
had any other spools of thread with which she might
have mended the shirt. Nancy, utterly cooperative
with the kindly detective, went to another room and
brought back another spool.

Eventually the spools would be submitted to the
FBI lab in Washington, and a fibers expert there
would discover that in color, composition, thickness
—indeed, in every respect—the second spool
matched the thread that had been used to sew
Douglas's shirt.

The search turned up other extremely incriminating pieces of evidence. One was a box of plastic garbage bags that appeared to match, in size, color, and
brand, the bag that had been taken out of the rest
area trash barrel. Another was one of Robin's pocket-
books, which a trooper found in Douglas's bedroom

closet. It was stuffed with prophylactics. Robin's address book was also found, as was the beeper to her Panasonic answering machine, her Armstrong flute, and her pink panties.

But the most damaging piece of evidence was one that the police chemist, Ronald Kaufman, stumbled across. Searching the living room closet, he came upon a man's blue windbreaker. He did a presumptive test for blood on the windbreaker and found that there was a positive reaction in the right-hand pocket.

The jacket was confiscated. Later, it too would be sent to a lab for analysis, and it would turn out that in the right-hand pocket there was, not only a tiny smear of blood, but a fingernail-size piece of human brain tissue. The jacket was, of course, the one that Douglas had taken out of his closet right after killing Robin, in which he'd tried to conceal the hammer. Apparently he'd forgotten all about that effort.

Douglas wasn't arrested that night. But by the time the police left his home, they had discovered, not just Robin's personal effects and the blood-tinged windbreaker, but letters he had written to her, papers in which he'd spelled out her involvement in the Tufts swindle, and a page in her address book on which he'd made himself a note about a Joseph Murray in Charlestown. They took all these things with them. And they also took his telephone bills, gasoline receipts, and an Amtrak timetable.

It wasn't enough evidence to justify arresting the professor, who had maintained throughout the search that he knew nothing of Robin's disappearance and that someone, probably J.R., had planted her possessions in his home. To arrest Douglas, the police would first have to come up with strong proof of two separate contentions. One was that Robin Benedict was actually dead, not merely missing—a complicated proposition, since her body had not turned up. The other was that after Robin left Douglas's home on Saturday night, the professor hadn't gone to bed—as he kept insisting—but that he had gone somewhere else. Somewhere with Robin. Or her body. Still, the evidence that had been found was enough to get the police started.

And what of Douglas? How did he react to the fact that, despite his precautions, he was now under suspicion of murder? He seems to have believed that he could get away with the murder if only he were clever enough, and consequently devoted himself to his scheme of making it appear that Robin was still alive. In mid-March, neighbors above the last trick pad that she had rented heard someone playing the flute in her rooms. In April, on Easter Sunday, the Benedicts received a telegram signed "Robin," which said that she was alive and well and living in Las Vegas.

But while his arranging these ghostly acts was, under the circumstances, logical and understandable, the efforts of a suspect to throttle suspicion, Douglas also began to behave in illogical, unfathomable, and compulsive ways. Always, at least as far as anyone knew, a responsible scientist, he now started to produce—at a part-time job with Scott Laboratories in Rhode Island—unreliable work. He was doing experiments with cancer cells and coming up with interesting results, but his findings couldn't be duplicated by others. In science, this is almost always a worrisome signal, and late in April his supervisor accused him of confabulating his findings and dismissed him. Subsequently, he was reduced to taking a job as a desk clerk at the YMCA in Boston. But there, too, he behaved oddly. On one occasion he pretended to want to buy, but in fact temporarily absconded with, the automobile of a Y resident.

Something in him seemed to have snapped. He was out of control, a man who had lost his rudder, who had drifted far from the machinery of middle-class propriety which had previously kept him on course. He and Nancy were barely communicating. He took no interest in the children. And he began to turn up in the Combat Zone once again, there to pick up prostitutes and accompany them to trick pads or cheap motels or just into cars for quick sex. His sexual appetite was urgent, mechanical, seemingly insatiable. Lieutenant Sharkey, observing him from an unmarked car, noticed that on occasion he would climax with one prostitute and then, an hour later, find himself another and repeat the experience. He had become, like Tantalus, a man for whom there could be no satisfaction.

His life throughout this period was filled not only with sociopathy and satyriasis but with bitter ironies. He had used up all his savings back in the days before he'd begun stealing from Tufts. Now, the Hartford Accident and Indemnity Company, which had reimbursed Tufts for the losses he had caused, wanted to recover. They took a lien on his house. Needing money desperately, he began to work at any job he could find, no matter how demeaning. For a while he even did market research over the telephone. Then he looked for a job as a laborer, like his father before him, but found none. After a while, his circumstances were so straitened that he was reduced to picking up extra cash by scavenging for refundable cans and bottles.

* * *

While Douglas was spiraling ever downward, Sharkey and his men were making strides toward uncovering his actions on the night of the killing. Here they were helped by another irony, for even then Douglas had been so strapped for cash that he had used credit cards wherever he went. Obtaining his credit card bills, the police discovered that he'd bought gas in Boston that night and that he'd telephoned Nancy from a highway rest area near the one where the hammer was found, as well as from a Howard Johnson's in Pawtucket and a bus station in Providence. Clearly, whatever he claimed, the professor hadn't been home in bed that night.

Clearly, too, on the next night, he hadn't gone directly to Washington, as he'd insisted. Once again, because he'd used a credit card, the police were able to ascertain that he left for Washington not from Massachusetts but from New York City. On Sunday, March 6, he'd presented his card in New York's Pennsylvania Station to purchase an Amtrak ticket to Washington on a train leaving at 3:33 A.M.; Sharkey, sorting through boxes of ticket stubs at Amtrak headquarters, eventually found the very ticket that had been issued to Douglas.

"Mrs. Douglas," Sharkey said to Nancy one day in late April, "why don't you tell us where your husband was on the night Robin Benedict disappeared, and what he told you, so we can recover her automobile and body?" By this time he and his fellow officers had established that Douglas had lied to them about his movements, but they still didn't have enough evidence to prove beyond a shadow of a doubt that Robin had in fact been murdered. There was a tiny smear of blood and brain tissue in the pocket of Douglas's windbreaker. But there were no tests that could prove that the speck of tissue had come from the brain of Robin Benedict and no other. And while there were new and excellent tests for identifying victims through their blood, the amount of dried fluid found on the windbreaker was very small. William Delahunt, the district attorney of Norfolk County, was eager to have Robin's body itself or, failing that, at least some more substantial remains. But where to look?

Nancy, ever so wistful, ever so sad, deflected Sharkey's question. She couldn't talk, she told him; "I can't. I'm sorry. You would have to be married to a man for twenty years to understand."

Delahunt, an experienced district attorney—he had been Norfolk County's chief prosecutor for years—suspected that since Douglas had been in New York on Sunday, March 6, he might have disposed of Robin's body there. Other people connected with the case had more fanciful notions. Some believed that Douglas had dismembered Robin and, en route to New York, discarded bits and pieces of her body along the highway. After all, he was a professor of anatomy, wasn't he? Others believed that he might have cremated her body in the incinerator at Tufts Medical School. A Harvard Medical School professor had done just that back in the nineteenth century, murdering a colleague to whom he owed a debt, then incinerating the victim in his laboratory. There'd been nothing left of the man except a portion of his pelvic area with the male genitalia attached. Still others thought that most likely Robin's body had been placed in her car and the whole pushed into the waters off the coast. After all, it wouldn't be the first time a young woman had been found dead in that fashion in New England. Throughout the spring and early summer, divers from in and around Robin's hometown of Methuen made exhausting underwater searches for her car in the still-frigid waters.

By this time, the police were intensely eager to arrest Douglas. In Sharon, the body of a naked thirteen-year-old girl had been found in a sandpit. She had been killed by a blow from a blunt instrument to her head, and the crime had never been solved. In Plattsburgh, too, a girl had died under mysterious circumstances that were never resolved. Her death had occurred while Douglas was living there. The professor, the police worried, might be even more dangerous than a one-time murderer. He might turn out to be a serial killer, a stalker of girls and women. They wanted him off the streets, but without proof that Robin had been murdered their hands were tied.

Then, at last, they had a breakthrough. On July 16, in New York City, a policewoman on a routine patrol noticed a silver Toyota without plates parked on the street about a block from Pennsylvania Station. The policewoman ran the information through the computer at the station house, and a report came back. The car, said the report, might belong to a missing person named Robin Benedict who might have been the victim of a homicide in Norfolk County, Massachusetts.

Two Manhattan South Precinct homicide investigators were promptly dispatched to go to Penn Station and examine the automobile. They opened the door, and immediately a strong odor of decay assailed their nostrils. It was the unmistakable odor of decomposing human matter. "Once you've smelled it, you never forget it," one of the investigators told Manhattan reporters, describing how he and his partner, nauseated, had pushed back the seat of the Toyota and there, in the back of the car, observed a mass of pine needles matted with dried blood.

Sharkey and his men came right down to New York City. They needed to figure out where the car—it was definitely Robin's—had been before the police-woman spotted it and how long it had been in its previous location. They began interviewing the owners and employees of every parking garage in the area.

It took them several days of pounding the unfamil-iar Manhattan sidewalks, but after a stretch of round-the-clock interviews they had their answers. The silver Toyota had been parked in a garage called Myer's, directly opposite Penn Station, until, after months of not being able to determine the car's owner and collect a parking fee, attendants at Myer's shoved the car out of the garage. When had the car first been parked in the garage? On the evening of Sunday, March 6, the detectives learned.

In Boston, where the car itself had been returned, Kaufman, the chemist, went to work. He examined the car's bloodstained upholstery and deck mats and submitted them to the FBI laboratory in Washington, which already had the other bloodstained items from the trash barrel. And he came upon a less obvious find—another piece of what looked like human tis-sue. It was minuscule, no larger than the head of a pin, but perhaps it would be useful. Kaufman took the tissue and submitted it to a patholgist.

By the late summer of 1983, Delahunt's office had begun to weave a tight web around Douglas. The po-lice were still shadowing his every move. A special grand jury had been convened to hear testimony concerning the case, and efforts were under way to force Douglas's children to testify in front of that jury. Delahunt was speculating that they and their mother might have seen the killing, or at least the aftermath of it, when they arrived home that terrible night. Getting Nancy to describe what she had seen would be out of the question. By Massachusetts law, a wife can't be forced to testify against her husband. However, there is no law that children can't be made to testify against their parents, and Delahunt was determined to examine the Douglas children. What had *they* seen? What had *they* heard? A legal battle ensued, with the Douglases struggling to keep their children from having to give testimony and Delahunt's office struggling to force them to do so.

Ultimately, the prosecution won the legal struggle, but even before that happened, Delahunt's confidence that he could win a murder conviction against Douglas grew, for at last his office was informed that the blood in Robin's car was most likely hers. The FBI lab in Washington, using complex new genetic marker tests, had analyzed the stains on the upholstery and deck mats of the Toyota and compared them with blood samples taken from Shirley and John Benedict and Robin's four siblings. The blood in the car was composed of precisely the same elements as that of the rest of the family.

Finally the pathologist to whom Kaufman had submitted the tiny bit of tissue he'd found in the car turned in his report. The tissue was white matter, from the inner or deeper part of the brain.

The evidence that Robin was dead, and that she had been hammered to death, was now quite conclusive. And it certainly appeared that her killer was the esteemed professor, William Douglas.

On October 28, 1983—nearly eight months after the killing—Douglas was arrested while driving into Cambridge, informed that he was being indicted for the murder of Robin Benedict, and taken to the police station in Sharon. He asked to make two calls. One was to his wife, who seemed not to believe him when he told her where he was, for he kept saying, "Honest, honest," and "Really, I'm not kidding." The other was to his current employer, an automobile rental agency where he was working as a car jockey. In an orderly fashion, he gave his boss a long list of the whereabouts of the various cars he had been supposed to pick up that day. Interestingly, he called his boss before he called his wife.

Family Units

"This is a case of the Commonwealth of Massachusetts versus William Douglas. The charge against Mr. Douglas is murder." Over and over the words droned on as Judge Roger Donahue of the Massachusetts Superior Court began examining prospective jurors in the graceful, nineteenth-century county courthouse in Dedham, Massachusetts, the last week of April 1984. Donahue had recorded the questions he wanted to ask the jurors, and a clerk kept rewinding the cassette as each sober-faced citizen was led into the austere, paneled room. "Would your judgment be affected by the fact that there was a close relationship between the defendant, a married man, and Robin Benedict, a single person?" the tape recorder eerily kept demanding. "Would your judgment be affected by the fact that Robin Benedict, or any witness in this case, was a prostitute?"

I settled down in the courtroom, feeling lucky to have a seat, for the rows reserved for the press were jammed. Years before, Sacco and Vanzetti had been tried in this same tranquil courthouse, and virtually every newspaper in the country had sent reporters to cover the trial. It looked as if the story of the professor and the prostitute was going to run Sacco and Vanzetti a close second. Indeed, the case had received so much publicity already that Donahue was having a difficult time finding jurors who could answer no to the recorded question "Have you heard or learned anything about this case from the news media or any other source?"

Because of this problem, one afternoon Donahue began taking a more aggressive tack with prospective jurors who thought they already knew whether or not Douglas had killed Robin. Trying to explain to them that despite whatever they had heard or read, they ought nevertheless to be able to render a fair and impartial verdict, he lectured them: "In our system, cases are decided on the basis of evidence." Then he asked whether those jurors who were already familiar with the case thought they could put their preconceptions out of their minds and arrive at a conclusion based on the evidence that would be presented in court.

Many doubted that they could.

My eyes wandered toward Douglas. He was seated at the defendant's table between his counsel, Thomas C. Troy, and Troy's assistant, William J. Doyle, and all week, extremely agitated, he had been tapping his fingers on the table or playing with a pen, resting it in one hand while repeatedly rubbing his fingers along its length with the other. Now, I noticed, he was scribbling a note to himself.

What had Douglas written? I asked Doyle during a break. Doyle smiled perplexedly and said, "It's the same thing he writes whenever he makes notes. He keeps writing, 'There must be a way.'"

Douglas was the only person who believed it. Troy and Doyle were familiar with the impressive case the prosecution was planning to present. Delahunt's office had given the defense its witness list, a scroll that contained more than 150 names. Among them were the names of telephone company supervisors, who would assert that their records indicated that Douglas had not been asleep in bed during the hours after Robin had been to see him, and those of serological specialists, who would testify that a bit of Robin's brain had been found in Douglas's windbreaker. Delahunt had picked, to argue the State's case, John Kivlan, one of his most meticulous assistants, a man known to be so relentless at cross-examination that he had earned from his fellow prosecutors the nickname "the Aggressor." Troy and Doyle had little optimism about being able to win the case for Douglas.

They were the sixth team of lawyers to attempt to defend him. The others had either been dismissed by Douglas for a variety of reasons, ranging from incompetence to lack of rapport, or had themselves relinquished the case because, or so the courthouse gossip went, the professor couldn't pay their high fees. Troy had been appointed by the court.

It was rumored that he had accepted largely because the case would bring him vast publicity. He is, like so many defense attorneys, an outgoing, histrionic man who thoroughly enjoys the theater—and the attendant notices—of murder trials. The son of a Boston police detective who had been killed while making an arrest, Troy had followed in his father's footsteps, become a cop, and only much later, as a result of an on-the-job injury that limited his ability to perform a policeman's active work, decided to go to law school. By the time he graduated, his fondness for attracting media attention was clear. On the day he passed his bar examination, he hired a helicopter and had it land smack in the middle of Boston's District Court area.

There was no question but that Troy had been looking forward to the publicity that the trial of William Douglas was going to command. But by the week of jury selection, he had begun hoping that Douglas wouldn't insist on letting the trial run its course. The colorful attorney had an astonishingly unblemished record as a defense attorney, having won each one of the fifty-five murder cases he had tried prior to that week. And it wasn't just his own record he wanted to protect. It was Douglas's future. If Douglas was tried and convicted of premeditated murder, he could be sentenced to life in prison. If he pleaded guilty, he could conceivably get off with as few as five years. Throughout the long week of jury selection, Troy kept reasoning with his client that it would be best if he pleaded guilty. But Douglas, arguing with his attorney, writing notes to himself about how there must be a way, refused to take a plea.

* * *

What finally made him change his mind? I suspect it was studying the faces of the men and women who were, ever so slowly, being selected as jurors. They were, for the most part, married and the parents of several, generally teenaged, children. By Thursday afternoon, April 26, 1984, they had all been chosen, and Donahue announced that the trial would commence the next morning. I suspect that Douglas had been feeling an impending sense of doom as each middle-aged family man or woman was sworn in. Although by legal definition they were people equal to him in rank and standing, he must have realized that they were nothing like him at all. He had always been estranged from ordinary men and women. In any event, that afternoon, as soon as the court had adjourned for the day, he asked Troy to indicate to the district attorney's office that he was at long last willing to confess, providing the charge against him could be reduced from murder to manslaughter.

I didn't know about these behind-the-scenes negotiations, nor did any of the journalists covering the Douglas case. We had all been taking bets about whether the trial was going to be a four-week affair or a six-week marathon, and most of us, convinced that one way or the other this would be our last free afternoon for a long time, left Dedham in a hurry, eager to attend to other things.

I went to see some of the sites that would be mentioned in the trial: Robin's home in Malden, Douglas's home in Sharon. Both houses looked deserted, their windows shut, their shades and curtains drawn. On the Douglas lawn, a rusty bicycle was lying on its side, one wheel jutting upward, as if it had been abruptly abandoned by someone hastily called from play and never again interested in returning to it. I have no idea to whom the bicycle belonged or how long it had been lying there, but at that moment William Douglas's children suddenly became real to me, and I found myself shivering in the warm spring sunshine. Until then, I'd thought of the story as a tragedy for Douglas. I'd forgotten that a father's tragedy is never his alone.

The following morning, I arrived in Dedham a good hour before the trial was due to start, but the courtroom was already packed. Spectators and press people jostled one another, hurrying toward seats as if down the aisles of a movie that had already begun. But nothing happened for what seemed like hours. The judge had instructed everyone to arrive by 9:30 A.M. so that the trial could start promptly, but now there was no sign of him nor of the carefully chosen jurors. The spectators fidgeted. Reporters scribbled notes about the fidgety spectators. Finally, there was a noise at a side door to the courtroom, and at last the principals in the trial hurried to their places. Judge Donahue took the bench. John Kivlan strode to the prosecutor's table. William Douglas, accompanied by defense attorney Troy, moved lumberingly to the defense side of the room.

But no jurors appeared. And now, filing into the courtroom in place of the jury, were some of the people who were to have been witnesses at the trial as well as Robin Benedict's parents, her four siblings, Richard, Rhonda, Robert and Ronald, and Clarence ("J.R.") Rogers. Incredibly, since after all it was supposedly J.R. who had introduced their daughter to prostitution and thus, indirectly, to her killer, the Benedicts had formed a close attachment to J.R. during the course of the investigation. Now they chatted with him as they maneuvered into a row and put him between them. But, once seated, J.R. no longer spoke to them. He just kept staring icily at Douglas's back. Something was clearly afoot.

A few seconds later, without further ado, John Kivlan began speaking: "Your Honor, I wish to advise you that Mr. Troy has advised me this morning that the defendant Douglas wishes to change his plea from not guilty to guilty to so much of the indictment that alleges he did assault and beat Robin Benedict and did kill Robin Benedict, that is, to so much of the indictment as alleges manslaughter."

Whispers of astonishment, whoops of amazement, even quickly muffled applause, spread through the courtroom, and a few minutes later Judge Donahue began addressing Douglas. Did he understand that by pleading guilty, he might receive not a short sentence but as much as eighteen to twenty years?

He did.

Did he understand what manslaughter was? That it referred to a killing committed either through reckless conduct or in the heat of passion—whether anger, fear, fright, or nervous excitement?

He did.

"And did you kill Robin Benedict?" Judge Donahue asked.

"Yes," William Douglas said.

I was even more startled by what transpired next. Kivlan was reviewing for the assemblage the evidence the State would have presented when suddenly Douglas asked permission to speak.

It was granted. He stood. His voice quavery, he began to apologize. He said how sorry he was for having taken up the time of the judge: "I understand and I know that you are a very, very busy person and I have misued a lot of your time." But, he went on to say, it wasn't just to the judge that he really wished to apologize. It was to Robin's parents. "I would like, with your permission, to address the Benedict family," he requested of Donahue. And then he added, humbly, "Although I don't really have the right."

Suddenly a terrifying sound erupted from the back of the courtroom. It was a snarl, a sound of rage so loud it could be heard in every corner. J.R. had started to his feet and was shouting, "Fuck you!"

Douglas turned pale and seemed to shake. But clearly he wanted his moment of penitence desperately, for he went on, almost without missing a beat: "I know Mr. and Mrs. Benedict and they are fine people. They have raised a wonderful family unit."

I felt that in Douglas's very choice of words there was something peculiar, disconnected, the sound of the observer and the stranger. Robin's parents had raised, not a family, but a "unit." J.R. and the Benedicts must have felt a chill like my own, for J.R. screamed, "Shut up," and Mrs. Benedict burst into tears.

It was to be a long while before I understood all that had happened between Douglas and Robin, all that had characterized the professor's emotional life. But when I did, it occurred to me that his mea culpa in the courtroom was something to which all the other apologies in his life had been leading up—the apologies to his parents for not being a good enough boy, the apologies to Nancy for not being a good enough husband, the apologies to Robin for not being able to stop being a pest and a nag. Surely that was why he spun out his apology to the judge and the

Benedicts, repeating the same words, talking on and on, refusing to be done with it.

When he finished apologizing to the judge and the Benedicts, Douglas apologized to his wife and children.

Ten days later, on May 7, 1984, fourteen months after the killing, William Douglas was sentenced. During the days that intervened, he made his two-day confession and, at the request of the district attorney's office, gave elaborate details about the location of the dumpster into which he had thrown Robin's body. Attorney Troy, pointing out how cooperative he'd been, asked the court to impose a minimum sentence—five to fifteen years in prison. Bill Douglas, he said, was a "gentle, sensitive, educated man" who had "left the Alice-in-Wonderland world of academia" only to be ensnared by "the world of sex, extortion, violence, larceny, the world of prostitutes and pimps [who] reached out and consumed him."

Kivlan asked for the maximum sentence—eighteen to twenty years. He had read Douglas's confession and found in it evidence that Douglas had calculated Robin's death, not merely killed her in a moment of sudden passion. "This is not a kind man," he said. "This is not a gentle man easily led astray by beautiful young women. This is a devious, mature man, an intelligent, calculating man who knew what he was doing."

Judge Donahue seemed to concur. He sentenced Douglas to eighteen to twenty years, and moments later the professor, his expression astonishingly youthful and vulnerable, his hands manacled, his arms clutching his worn, overstuffed scholar's briefcase, was led away.

* * *

That afternoon, Robin's parents held a press conference in Methuen. Nancy Douglas had given a statement to the press the previous day, saying, "Bill was everything I ever wanted in a husband and father... I still love him," and now, not to be outdone, the Benedicts talked of their love. "No matter what has been learned about our daughter's secret life," they said, "we'll always love her." But I left the conference thinking that the crime, and the investigation, had—whatever they said—reduced that love. How could it not? Robin's parents had had to accommodate to a new vision of their daughter. They'd known she had sex for money, but—or so they said—they'd been privy to none of the details of her days, her drug habit, her extremely active hustling, her alleged extortionism. To them, Robin had still been a promising, talented girl, and they'd assumed that prostitution was, for her, a phase, a stage, a rebellion, something she'd soon grow out of.

I felt, as I rode back to Boston that afternoon, that one of the sad things about murder is that, inevitably, not just the perpetrator but the victim is probed, revealed, exposed. Murder takes away not only life but reputation, thereby doubly robbing a victim's family.

Douglas was sent to the Massachusetts state correctional facility at Walpole. J.R. left town. And Tom Troy and William Delahunt, no longer antagonists, arranged to get together for a couple of beers.

Interestingly, Robin's body never turned up. Trooper Brian Howe went down to Providence to talk with trash collectors there. He learned that the garbage in the dumpsters in the shopping mall where Douglas had discarded Robin's body was routinely

compacted and used for landfill in a large land recla-
mation site in Jamestown, Rhode Island. But no one
connected with the site could tell him exactly where,
or how deep, in the hundred-acre area the garbage
collected on Sunday, March 6, 1983, might be. Moreover, Howe learned that the garbage would have been
routinely crushed by a trash compactor, which would
most likely have eliminated much of the body's bone
matter, and that even if some of Robin's bones had—
miraculously—emerged intact from the compactor,
they would have been exposed to ground shifting and
animal activity in the landfill. These actions would
have caused separation of the skeletal remains.

Howe came back to Dedham recommending that
no further search be undertaken, for it would surely
prove futile. It had turned out that Douglas's choice of
a method for getting rid of a body had, indeed, been a
choice worthy of a professor.

A year later I was still doing research, still tying up
loose ends, and I went back to New England for a few
days. I stayed in a dreary hotel where Robin used to
pick up traveling businessmen, did some last-minute
interviews, visited the Combat Zone again, and one
afternoon went to Dedham to talk with the police and
lawyers at the district attorney's office there about
what they thought, finally, about the case and the sort
of man Douglas really was.

I met that day with Lieutenant Sharkey, Trooper
Howe, District Attorney Delahunt, Assistant District
Attorney Kivlan, and another district attorney whom
I'd never seen before, Matt Connolly. Sharkey said
he'd believed Douglas about the hammer's having
been brought into his house by Robin and that he still

believed it. Kivlan said he hadn't believed it at the time of the confession and still didn't.

Sharkey said, "You want to know what kind of a guy Douglas was? He's the wimp everyone went to school with, the little fat kid who couldn't tie his own shoes, the one who, if you threw him a basketball, he dropped it, the one with his arms sewed on backward." Connolly said, "No, he was smarter than that. Wilier. He wanted us to think he was just a wimp, but I think he planned her killing, and that he planned it cleverly." Someone murmured, "Except for the credit cards. That wasn't smart."

What about the two unsolved murders that they'd been worried about when Douglas was on the loose? I asked them.

"You read his confession," Sharkey said. "We probed him about those deaths, but he denied knowing anything about them." Connolly spoke up: "I don't believe him. I think he could have been connected to them." He was working on the Sharon case, but so far he'd failed to find anything to link the professor to it.

I didn't think Douglas was involved. The police had found no evidence, when they searched his house, of his ever having loved another girl besides Robin, no frilly mementos of some other female, no lonesome, longing letters to anyone but her. Douglas, I felt certain, and said to Connolly, had been in love just that one time, and he had killed Robin only because she had exploited, then rejected, his love.

That night on the plane back to New York, I reread some of Douglas's letters to Robin. "Dear," went one, "Since I have known you, I have always tried to be by your side in time of need. Now I desperately need

some help from you!" It was the letter he had written
to her just after he'd been let go by Tufts, one of the
many she hadn't answered. "I am so alone. I need to
be able to reach you or talk with you," the letter continued. "Please don't turn yourself away from me
now.... I need you, dear." It certainly sounded like
love, I thought. Gave the appearance of love. But suddenly I began to ask myself, was it really love? Is not
love the feeling that someone else's well-being is as
important to the self as one's own? And does not that
feeling require that one understand that one's partner
is someone else, and just who he or she is?

It was clear to me then, concentrating on the
words and at last considering all I knew about
Douglas and Robin, that Douglas had never really
understood who Robin was, not even in the first days
of their "affair." He had formed an attachment, not to
an actual girl, but to a figment of his imagination. No
wonder he'd felt he could erase her, wipe her away. In
my mind's eye, I kept seeing him wrapped with Robin
in their final embrace, arms and legs tangled together
on the king-size bed, the hammer over their heads,
and I thought Douglas had killed, not someone he
loved, but someone he had loved having invented.

FROM A NICE FAMILY

Dallas, Texas

1981

I hadn't spent much time in Texas when I accepted an assignment to go to Dallas to investigate the story of a fourteen-year-old boy who had shot his mother and father to death. Oh, I'd been to Texas. I'd flown in and out of both Houston and Dallas on book tours, but I'd never stayed long enough to make friends. I didn't know anything except what I'd read and heard from Texas friends who'd come east about the extraordinary hospitality with which their countrymen treat visitors—and the extraordinary casualness with which they treat guns.

One of my transplanted Texas friends said as I was leaving New York, "You'll love Texas. But make sure you don't jaywalk. You'll notice that no one ever jaywalks in Dallas."

"Why not?" I asked, ever the straight man.

"Because if they do, they're liable to get shot. Either by the police or by some law-abiding citizen who doesn't like to see the rules get broken."

Another Texas friend living in New York said, "What, another kid killing his mama and papa? Well, it'll turn out like the classic story of the guy who kills his folks, then begs the court for mercy because he's an orphan. Only, since this is Texas, they'll see his point."

I chided both my friends for painting their home-
land so stereotypically. And I set off for ten days in
Dallas, where, to my astonishment and delight, I was,
as Henry James might say, taken up. I was invited to
dinners in sophisticated restaurants, to catered backyard barbecues, to art openings, concerts, a poetry
reading. I fell in love with Texas because all the
Texans I met were so friendly, so warm and person-
able. But an astonishing number of my new acquain-
tances admitted to me that they had guns. "You need
'em out here," was the usual explanation. No matter
that "out here" was, increasingly, tracts of suburban
homes, mile after mile of sprinkler-showered lawn.
Texans don't seem to recognize that the state is no
longer a wilderness, or at least that the wilderness
that grows in the hearts of men might never burgeon
and blossom and become untamable if guns weren't a
household item, as expected as mesquite chips and
pickup trucks.

The story I'd come to report on was that of David
Keeler, whose mother, Anita, had been a superb
homemaker and whose father, Bill, had been president of Arco Oil and Gas. David had shot them one
Sunday morning in the summer of 1981 as they returned home from church.

I got the details of the crime by going, first, to see
Jim Gholston, a detective on the Dallas police force.
Gholston told me, "These cases where a kid goes
crazy and knocks off his parents are terrible. We've
had a few of them lately. This one was particularly
gruesome. The boy confronted his folks outside their
bedroom and shot them each several times. The father died right away, but the mother, well, she was
riddled with bullet holes but she lasted several hours.
Long enough to say who did it."

Gholston shook his head. A big man and a soft-spoken one, he was dressed that afternoon in a white-on-white cowboy shirt with silvery snaps up the cuffs and a large, ornate brass belt buckle. He was also wearing a studded brass holster and a gun with an ornate pearl handle. I'd interviewed dozens of police detectives in New York, but I'd never seen a policeman display his gun in front of a reporter and I'm afraid I stared a bit, but he seemed not to mind. Getting out a file, he read me a description of David: "Blond. Blue-eyed. Five feet, eight inches. One hundred and thirty-seven pounds."

Gholston seemed to have sympathy for both the parents and the child, saying, "They're dead, but in a way, his life is lost now, too."

What made him do it? I wanted to know.

"It's hard to say. There didn't seem to be any major problems, nothing other than the usual raising-a-teenager problems. In fact, what we seem to have here is a pretty well model child and a pretty well model family. It makes funny things go through your mind."

Like what? I asked him.

His forehead wrinkled. "I can't tell you the percentage of homes in Texas that have guns in them. That's what goes through your mind. That, and your own home."

Why? Did he keep guns around?

"Well, not out in the open," he said. "I'm careful where I keep them. But of course, with me being a police office, there are weapons around the house."

When I was leaving, he told me he had a fifteen-year-old son.

I had a similar conversation later that day with Jim Shivers, a police officer with Dallas's Youth Services, who'd interviewed David Keeler a few hours after the shooting. The boy had been cooperative and polite, Shivers told me. Then he too looked uneasy as he said, "I have a kid the same age. You couldn't ask for my kid to be more polite. It's yes-sir and no-sir all the time." He shuddered. "I guess it was the gun."

How come the Keelers had a gun? I asked.

He looked at me blankly, as if I'd asked an incomprehensible question. Then, "They were outdoors people," he said.

Gholston and Shivers weren't the only Dallas parents to find in what had happened to the Keelers cause for a kind of personal anxiety. The Reverend Charles W. Cook, minister of the Schreiber United Methodist Church, where the Keelers and many of their neighbors worshiped, told me that his congregation was obsessed with the Keeler killing. He said, "The parents keep saying, 'Such a nice family. Such a good boy. Could my child ever turn on me?' And the children keep asking, 'Could I ever do such a thing to my parents?' A lot of the families have guns, but they haven't thrown them away."

Of course, it wasn't just because of the gun that David Keeler had killed his parents. I was to learn that there'd been a long-standing feud in the Keeler family, a war between the parents and the child that began once David became an adolescent and wanted to do things his way. Still, until that time and even after they grew embittered and embattled, the Keelers had seemed like an average enough family, a happy enough family. It was this aspect of the crime that frightened the congregation of the Schreiber United Methodist Church and many of the people who knew, or came to know, members of the family.

I heard a good deal about how happy they'd all seemed from a colleague of Bill Keeler's named Stuart Mut, a senior vice president at Arco's parent company, the Atlantic Richfield Corporation. Mut had known the Keeler family for some thirty years and David for his entire life. "They were a well-balanced bunch," he said. "The parents were sincerely interested in the kids. The boy wasn't temperamental or anything."

We were sitting in Mut's icy, air-conditioned office high above the streets of Dallas, and he went on to tell me about Bill and Anita. Bill had started out quite modestly. He'd been born in Brownwood, Texas, a small, arid town in the western part of the state, and studied engineering at Texas A&M. After a stint in the navy, he'd joined Atlantic Richfield in 1949 as a junior engineer and worked there the rest of his life, slowly shouldering his way through the corporate ranks to hold down ever more complex and responsible positions. In 1973, he'd made it to vice president in charge of research and engineering. And in the spring of 1981, shortly before his son killed him, he'd been named president of Arco, Atlantic Richfield's largest subsidiary. "He was a strong but quiet man," Mut said. "He had all the standard engineer's characteristics. He was logical and analytical in his approach. But he also had a good feel for the other factors involved in an enterprise, for the human factors." Then, although I hadn't asked, he added, "Not the kind of man who would ever bully anybody."

Anita Keeler was a homebody, although she too had excellent organizational skills. She raised four children: Barbara, who was in her late twenties, worked for the Environmental Protection Agency; John, who was twenty-five, was married and had a

son of his own; Robert, nineteen, was a student at the
University of Texas in Austin; and then there was
David, "the baby." Anita was an expert cook and
housekeeper. And, like Bill, who was fond of duck
hunting, she was a good shot. Just that year, she'd
bagged a deer and a turkey.

"The Keelers did a lot of hunting and fishing and
camping," Mut said. "Summers, at least when the
kids were little, the entire family would go camping at
Lake Ouachita in Arkansas. I used to take my wife
and kids there, too, so I had plenty of occasion to
watch the interaction of this family. And what I saw
was that they always seemed to be having fun, and
taking the greatest joy from their trips and being together."

The memory puzzled him. "You know," he went
on, "some people have asked whether perhaps the
Keelers were too strict with their children. Well, if
there's one time or place when you'd expect to see
parents bossing children around, it's on a camping
trip, where there are so many chores to be done and
when, especially if you've got a big brood, the kids
have to be kept in line. But I never saw anyone in that
family bossing anyone else around."

Still, the Keelers had stern ideas. For example,
they were great believers not just in the fun of out-
door life but in the way such a life could temper children, condition them. "At some point in her
development," Mut reminisced, "the Keelers' daughter, Barbara, apparently had some difficulties, as so
many adolescents do. Attacks of shyness, I think it
was. The Keelers enrolled her in one of those Outward Bound programs." Mut thought it was a good
idea. "I hear it helped. She became more self-confident."

I heard more about the Keelers from their neighbors on their quiet, lawn-lined street in North Dallas, a street of expensive but not opulent homes, with large yards and swimming pools behind. Lynda Avant, a neighbor who'd known the family for some ten years, told me that Anita Keeler involved herself tirelessly in community work: the PTA, Meals on Wheels, the United Methodist Women. If an after-school sports group needed equipment, Anita Keeler was the person who could be counted on to get merchants to contribute supplies. If a shut-in needed groceries, Anita Keeler was the person who could be counted on to make sure the food arrived promptly. If a handicapped student couldn't get to school on his own, Anita Keeler was the person who could be counted on to see that he got there, sometimes organizing friends to do the driving, sometimes taking on the onerous daily back-and-forth effort herself. The summer she was shot, she'd been ferrying a boy confined to a wheelchair to his classes at a community college in nearby Brookhaven. But Anita's interests in charitable work outside the home never kept her from being involved in her children's lives and activities, Avant told me. When Barbara was little, Anita served as a Campfire Girl leader. When the boys were growing up, she learned to be a sports fan. And she went to so many of David's games over at St. Mark's that the school newspaper remarked on her loyalty in an article and dubbed her "Superfan."

Bill Keeler was just as devoted. Despite the heavy demands of his career, he managed to see his boys play ball whenever he could. Sometimes, on his way home from a business trip, briefcase still in hand, he'd go directly from the Dallas airport to a school ball game. Other times, when one of the boys was playing a game out of town, he would fly out to watch him, even if the game was hundreds of miles away, in Houston or in Oklahoma.

Lynda Avant had a son the same age as David, and the two boys were the best of friends. They'd gone to the same schools, played on the same teams, done their Halloween trick-or-treating together every fall. "David was so cute and shy when he was little," she recalled. "I'll never forget the first time he came to dinner at our house. We were having English peas, and he didn't like them. So instead of eating them, he hid them under his plate. He didn't want to have to say he didn't like them. He was so sweet-looking then, with a little squared-off haircut. But he never went through the unkempt stage. He was the kind of little boy who never needed you to come along and tuck in his shirt for him."

David had been a conscientious and unusually well behaved child. And to some extent he remained this way, even when he reached adolescence and the war between him and his parents erupted. At the exclusive St. Mark's School of Texas, where he studied until he killed his parents, he'd maintained a B average, been on the Honor Roll, and become a member of the student council. A good athlete, he'd played on the football team. A good musician, he'd joined the school band, his instrument a second-hand top-of-the-line Bach trombone, which he paid for himself out of pocket money earned by mowing neighbors' lawns.

"He was one of our best and brightest," George Edwards, headmaster of St. Mark's high school, which David would have been entering in the fall, told me. "I always found him to be a very responsible

person in both academic and social areas," said Bob
Kohler, headmaster of the middle school, from which
he had just graduated.

He was considered bright and responsible by his
neighbors as well. "I used him as a baby-sitter," said
one neighbor, who had a toddler. "Now, would I have
done that if there was anything wrong with him?
Would any mother?"

But although few people who knew David were
aware of it, he had begun to resent his parents bitterly. And in the spring of 1981, the resentment became dangerously intense. That spring two things
happened: Bill Keeler was named president of Arco,
and David graduated from the eighth grade. The two
events were landmarks in the lives of both father and
son. They were celebrated with parties and congratu-
lations. They produced for each one a new sense of
mastery and triumph. But they also spawned in each
one a new sense of rights and privileges. And the
rights and privileges to which father and son felt entitled were in direct conflict.

David, viewing himself now as mature, wanted to
be allowed to do what the other kids he knew did—to
listen to rock 'n' roll, have girlfriends, stay out later at
night. Bill, feeling himself increasingly in the public
eye, disapproved of these activities and wanted his
son to behave not just well but better than the other
kids. David began defying his father.

There were nights that spring that he didn't come
home until the early hours of the morning. There
were days when he slept late and did nothing all afternoon but lounge around listening to his stereo.

There is no indication that at this point in his life
he was a particularly bad kid, a backtalking, pot-
smoking hooligan. But his parents, devout and con-

servative, with their stern, character-building ideas, considered his behavior unseemly and intolerable. They gave David an early curfew, and they sent him to work at the church's Vacation Bible School. They also threatened to revoke his stereo privileges if he didn't shape up. And they began to nag him, criticizing his hair—a full but not overly long rendition of the hair style popularized by the young John Kennedy—and his slothfulness, the fact that he was untidy and didn't make his bed in the mornings.

Their criticism simply strengthened his yearning to be free of supervision. He began slipping out of the house whenever he could.

But if David was defying his parents, he was not totally disobedient. That July he worked not only at the church school but as a counselor at St. Mark's day camp. He mowed lawns and baby-sat in order to earn pocket money for a backpacking trip to Alaska on which his parents had promised to send him. He attended to the household chores they assigned him— the care and cleaning of the backyard swimming pool and the care and feeding of the family schnauzer and his own pet, an orange-and-white-striped cat named Flash. And he never let on, at least not in the presence of any adults, that he was furious with his parents.

His ability to keep things to himself—ironically, it was a trait he'd learned from his father, who saw self-control as a sign of masculinity—may have been his undoing. According to his brother John, he was bottled up, choking on his anger. "He never talked back or argued," he said. "If he was reprimanded, he would just turn and go away."

But increasingly that summer he was reprimanded, and one day he did complain about it to a friend, a girlfriend. "My parents won't let me go where I want to go or do what I want to do," he told her.

Anita Keeler also complained. "David's turning out badly," she said to the Reverend Cook, beseeching him for advice.

Bill Keeler never complained—at least not outside his home. Every Saturday he played golf at the Brookhaven Country Club, and he never mentioned to any of his good friends there his struggle with his youngest son. Nor did he breathe a word about it to his friends at church, where every fourth Sunday he and Anita counted the collection money. But more and more Bill Keeler began to feel that his youngest son was a shame and a disgrace to him, and more and more he began to tell David this, shouting at him whenever they were in the privacy of their own home.

The Keelers may have been particularly uneasy about David because they felt disappointed in his brother John. John had run away from home right after high school and joined the army. When he'd come home, instead of going to college as the Keelers wanted, he'd fathered a child and gotten married. The Reverend Cook told me one afternoon, as we were sitting in his book-lined, tranquil study, "Anita Keeler brooded about this all the time, and was trying to blame someone or something for what had become of John. She'd say things like, 'If the church retreat had been properly chaperoned, all of this would never have happened.' By 'this,' she meant John's having a child when he was so young. I'd tell her that it was wrong to try to explain the direction of anyone's life by seeking the reason for that direction in this specific thing or that, and that it was wrong to brood over the past all the time. But it didn't do any good."

By July of 1981, Anita Keeler was unable to stop brooding. Bill Keeler was unable to get control of his youngest child. And David was unable to stop resenting his parents for what he considered their overbearing treatment of him.

At home, he retreated sullenly to his room. At church, which he still attended regularly, he became withdrawn.

"After services, I'm in the habit of standing in front of the church and saying goodbye to my parishioners, shaking hands and exchanging a few words," the Reverend Cook told me. "David wouldn't offer his hand. I'd always have to be the one to reach out. To try to touch him."

The restraint that had characterized both David and Bill Keeler began to crumble on Saturday night, July 11. That night David and three of his friends went to Six Flags Over Texas, a popular amusement park a few miles from the Keeler home. Waiting to ride on the Log Flume, the boys got rowdy and began cutting ahead through the line. Park security officers interceded and took the teenagers to the security office. There they discovered that the boys had in their possession a number of novelty items that they had shoplifted from amusement park vendors. The security police called the boys' families. Bill Keeler drove out to the park to take his son, and two of the other boys, home.

It must have been a frosty ride. It couldn't have been easy for a prominent corporate executive to fetch home a son accused of stealing. But Bill Keeler didn't reveal his anger in the car. Nor, in fact, did he reveal it once they reached home, for here, too, there were outsiders, Don Avant and his seventeen-year-old sister, Debra, come for a sleepover date because their parents were out of town. All that night, the Keelers kept up a front of calm and hospitality. Nothing was said about the Six Flags incident, and in the morning Anita Keeler insisted that the Avant children stay for breakfast; she made one of her elaborate spreads, stacks of pancakes and a sauté pan full of sausages. Perhaps she thought her son and her husband had put their anger aside. Or perhaps she was merely hoping to forestall an explosion between them. Whatever the reason, she prolonged breakfast, serving up seconds to the dawdling children. When Lynda Avant called to find out what her children were doing, Anita said cheerfully that everything was fine and they'd all be going swimming later in the day. Then Don and Debra ran home to change their clothes and get ready for church.

It was only then, in those few short minutes after the Avant children departed and before the Keelers and the Avants reconvened at the nearby church, that an argument erupted in the Keeler household. But when it did, it was savage. According to a sworn statement David was to give to the police, no sooner were his friends out the door than "my dad started yelling at me about the shoplifting. Mom was yelling with him. And he started to push me around a little, and grabbed me by the neck." Then, David went on, his father pushed him down the hall to his room, threw him on the bed, sat on him, and threatened to punch him.

Somehow, after that, Bill managed to get his anger under control, for he stood up and told David to hurry and get dressed for church. Even so, the Six Flags incident was not over. "As I was getting ready, they kept coming in and yelling at me about many things they said I had done," reported David, adding, "Most of which I hadn't."

Perhaps it was at this moment that the idea of killing his mother and father crept into the boy's mind. Or perhaps it was a few minutes later, as he sat in a pew in the church alongside them. Mr. Cook was giving a sermon about Jesus' parables, talking about the importance of stories in the lives of children. He spoke about how parents tell fairy tales to their kids, and how kids love to hear them, and how Jesus, like a fond parent, had tried to convey his teachings not with harshness but through the gentle medium of stories. David sat through the entire service. But when it was over, he bypassed the minister at the entrance to the church, slipping behind his back without a farewell. He headed home.

His parents, he knew, would be delayed because it was their turn to count the collection money. He went into the house and loaded his father's semiautomatic shotgun. When the Keelers entered the house fifteen minutes later, he was waiting for them in the foyer. He fired seven shots.

Barbara Keeler, who lived in her own apartment, arrived to go swimming in her parents' pool about a half hour later. She knocked on the door and, when no one answered, let herself in. She saw her mother lying in the hallway, groaning. Then, lifting her eyes, she stared down the hallway and saw her father. He, too, was lying on the floor, but no sound was coming from his lips.

She raced to him first, bending over him to see if

he was still breathing, but she could find no pulse or breath. She turned back to her mother, who was bleeding profusely. "David," moaned her mother. "David did it."

At that very moment David, dressed in a sweatshirt, shorts, and Adidas sneakers, was some four miles from the house, pedaling hard on his green Schwinn Varsity ten-speed. After the shooting, he had decided to run away; packing a bag, he tossed it into his bike basket and headed out of town. But suddenly a change came over him. Seeing a police car with two officers inside, he began to ride, almost automatically, toward it. As he drew close, one of the officers rolled down his window and looked at the boy casually, expecting to be asked directions.

"I just shot and killed my parents," David said.

He was taken to a Dallas police station, and there he talked about what he'd done and why. He'd killed his parents, he explained, because they'd been so strict, because they'd accused him of being a disgrace, and because his father had roughed him up and his mother had sided with his father.

"He talked quite freely," said Jim Shivers. "And he knew that what he'd done was wrong. But he was kind of emotionless. He had the same demeanor as if he'd been caught shoplifting."

Stuart Mot went over to the Keeler house that afternoon because he needed to discuss a business matter with Bill. He saw police cars surrounding the place and learned that the Keelers had been killed. He was stunned and, assuming his friends had been the victims of some vicious stranger, drove away. "We didn't learn until much later that day that it had been little David," he told me.

Lynda Avant went into the house once the bodies were removed. "The thing I remember best, the thing that gets me," she said, "was that on top of the washing machine I saw these new blue jeans Anita had just bought for David to take on his backpacking trip. She'd told me she was going to wash them for him before he wore them, to get the stiffness out. And alongside them on the top of the machine were those jingle bells that you wear on your ankles because of bears. She'd bought them and set them out so she could sew them on for him as soon as the jeans were washed."

The Reverend Cook also went over the house, then hurried down to the Dallas youth detention center to talk with David. "He was casual," he told me. "It was as if he was no different that night than he'd been when I'd seen him at church in the morning. He talked. But he said things like, 'I'm feeling okay' and 'It's been kind of a rough kind of day.'" Telling me about it, the minister had sighed and said, "Maybe he was in shock."

A few days after the shooting, the surviving members of the Keeler family hired for David a well-known, highly respected criminal lawyer named Doug Mulder. Under Texas law, youthful offenders—those under fifteen—could not at the time be charged and sentenced as adults. David's crime of patricide and matricide was considered a civil offense—delinquency—rather than a criminal one. But he could, if a judge so willed, be jailed for that delinquency in a juvenile detention center until he reached the age of eighteen. The family felt David would be better served by getting psychiatric treatment and consequently engaged the silver-tongued Mulder.

In August, at a hearing to determine what to do with David, Mulder produced a team of mental health experts who testified that intense criticism by his parents ever since he was a child had caused David to repress his emotions, and that this repression—rather like a fire in a coal mine that inevitably must seek the airshaft—had finally erupted into the violent rage that made the boy shoot to kill. He needed to be taught how to express his feelings, the experts felt, and how to do so constructively. The hearing was televised, and the judge sent David to a private psychiatric hospital, Timberlawn.

The Reverend Cook, when I spoke with him, several months after David had been sent to Timberlawn, said he was happy for the boy, although, like many people, he wasn't sure that psychiatric treatment could remake a personality. He also said that the members of the congregation had learned the wrong lesson from what had happened to the Keelers. "There is a mindset here that we're dealing with the will of God, that God caused all this to happen because in some way He was dissatisfied with us," the minister told me. "People here say, 'In the good old days, when everyone *believed*, you didn't have things like this.' Well, you did. What you didn't have then were guns, all those loaded guns. Those loaded guns in our homes are killing more of us than bad guys ever could. But people around here don't care."

David was treated at Timberlawn and then kept in a halfway house until late in 1984. By then I'd forgotten all about his case, but as I said, I'd made friends in Texas, and Texans are good about staying in touch.

That Christmas I got letters and cards from several of my Dallas friends, and one of them sent me a news clipping. David, the clipping said, would be released from psychiatric supervision on December 29—his eighteenth birthday. His juvenile record would be sealed. And he would receive his share of his parents' $1.2 million estate.

There was also a final twist, or at least what seemed to me to be a final nod to the anxieties that people living in a gun-toting society can never fully vanquish. The financial settlement had been negotiated among the Keebler siblings, who were apparently willing enough to give David his share of the family fortune. Interestingly, however, they stipulated that he not go to college either at the University of Texas in Austin or Southern Methodist University in Dallas, because of the two schools' proximity to them.

THE STRANGE DEATH OF THE TWIN GYNECOLOGISTS

New York, New York

1975

Above: Robin Benedict, the prostitute who exacted a high price from Douglas simply for her company (AP/Wide World Photos)

Top, left: William Douglas in court, before confessing to the murder of Robin Benedict (AP/Wide World Photos)

Bottom, left: Nancy, Douglas's wife of twenty years, on her way to court for his trial (Curtis Ackerman/*Boston Herald*)

David Keeler in 1981, shortly before he murdered both his parents (AP/Wide World Photos)

David's older brothers and sister *(from left to right),* John, Barbara, and Robert, at their parents' funeral (UPI/Bettmann Newsphotos)

MARCUS, C.

MARCUS, S.

Cyril Marcus *(top)* and Stewart Marcus, from a 1954 class
photograph from the SUNY Upstate Medical Center in
Syracuse, New York (AP/Wide World Photos)

The model student: Gerard Coury's yearbook picture (UPI/Bettmann Newsphotos)

Top, left: The house in Torrington, Connecticut, where Coury grew up (Jody Caravaglia)

Above: Coe Park in Torrington, Connecticut, where Coury took to loitering shortly before his final trip to New York City [Jody Caravaglia]

Dr. Robert Schwartz *(center)* at the funeral of his wife and two children (Ted Cowell)

The luxury apartment building on East 89th Street in New York where Irene Schwartz and her family lived until she shot herself and her two young children (Daniel Ribner)

Robyn Arnold, posing in front of Bloomingdale's in 1982 (J. Ross
Baughman/Visions)

Margaret Kilcoyne's passport photograph, as broadcast on television after her disappearance (*Boston Globe,* via Channel 3 Island Television, Nantucket)

The Nantucket house to which Dr. Kilcoyne retreated before she vanished (Peter Simon)

Right: John Buettner-Janusch at home, before he was convicted of making illegal drugs in his NYU laboratory (Deborah Feingold)

Bottom, right: Dr. Clifford Jolly in Buettner-Janusch's lab, where he helped unmask the drug scheme (Jody Caravaglia)

Frank Magliato at Riker's Island, following his conviction for the killing of Anthony Giani (©Donal F. Holway)

In the summer of 1975, a pair of forty-five-year-old twins, their bodies gaunt and already partially decomposed, were found dead at a fashionable Manhattan address in an apartment littered with decaying chicken parts, rotten fruit, and empty pill bottles. The bodies were those of Cyril and Stewart Marcus, doctors who had apparently died, more or less simultaneously, as the result of a suicide pact.

Like many people, I was shocked by the information. Two things contributed to my astonishment. One was the men's twinship, the doubleness that had given them a mutual birth date and now a mutual death date as well. Another was the men's prominence; they had been among New York City's most well-known obstetrician-gynecologists.

But if I was shocked, I was at the same time not surprised to hear of the death of the Marcus brothers, for I had known them, had once been a patient of Stewart Marcus. It was back in 1966, a year during which I paid several visits to his office but then abruptly decided not to continue seeing him. Though he was garrulous and even oddly confiding on one of my first two visits, on my third, he got angry about something—I no longer recall exactly what it was— and began to shout and scream at me. My husband was with me at the time, and I remember how, controlling an urge to respond in kind, he turned to me and said, "Let's go. This man is obviously crazy." Dr. Marcus seemed not to hear my husband's derogatory remark, though it was made sharply and loudly. He just went on ranting and raving, and we felt that although the doctor was standing just across his desk from us, it was as if, in effect, he were somewhere else, somewhere very distant. We stood up and left.

No doubt it was because of that experience— when I had so clearly perceived the gynecologist's distance from life, from reality—that I wasn't altogether surprised to hear of his and his brother's peculiar death. Indeed, a part of me wondered how anyone that disturbed and provocative had managed to function, cope, *survive* as long as he had. Nevertheless, I was immensely curious about how he had died, especially since there were a number of mysteries about what had occurred.

One mystery concerned the specific cause of death. A large number of empty barbiturate bottles were found in the apartment, and at first the medical examiner had assumed that the brothers had killed themselves by taking an overdose of sleeping pills. But autopsy tests revealed no trace of barbiturates in either body. The medical examiner's office next concluded that the twins had died from an attempted withdrawal from barbiturates. Such withdrawal can, in the case of chronic barbiturate addicts—and by this time it had been established that both twins had been taking mammoth doses of Nembutal for years— be as fatal as the addiction itself by producing life-threatening seizures and convulsions. After the M.E.'s report, however, some experts questioned the finding, since the bodies showed none of the typical signs that accompany death by convulsion, such as bruises, tongue bites, and brain hemorrhaging. New tests were performed, and this time it was discovered that in Stewart's body, at least, there *were* barbiturate traces, but not in Cyril's. How Cyril had died remained a puzzle.

Another mystery was that Cyril had outlived his brother by several days. Police investigators learned that he had even left the apartment once Stewart was dead, only to return and die alongside him. Why had he left? And why, for that matter, had he come back?

I began my investigation by talking, first, with police at the 19th Precinct, a few blocks from my home. Detectives from that precinct had been called to the apartment in which the twins had died—it was Cyril's apartment on York Avenue in the East Sixties —after a building repairman discovered the bodies. A lieutenant described to me the scene the detectives had encountered. "There wasn't an inch of floor that wasn't littered," he said. "The place was a pigsty." He went on to explain that one of the twins had been found lying face down across the head of a twin bed, the other, face up on the floor next to a matching twin bed in a different room. The features of the one on the bed—Stewart, dead longer than his brother— had already begun to decompose.

"Not a pretty sight," the lieutenant said. I nodded. "You want to see the pictures?" I said yes. But I couldn't bring myself to look at the bodies. I concentrated instead on the rooms themselves, vast seas of garbage, of unfinished TV dinners and half-drunk bottles of soda, of greasy sandwich wrappers and crumpled plastic garment covers. "See the chair." The lieutenant pointed at an armchair I'd hardly noticed,

a-swim in the debris. "See what's in the middle of it?"
I peered but couldn't tell. "That's because you've
probably never seen an armchair full of feces before."
The lieutenant guffawed. Then, serious and indig-
nant, he said, "They used the chair for their toilet!
Would you believe it!"

What I remember best about that encounter is that
when I got up to leave, I noticed tacked to the back of
the door a large print of the picture with the armchair. "A couple of the guys had it blown up," the
lieutenant, seeing me stare at it, explained. The pile
of excrement in the center of the chair had been cir-
cled with a wax pencil, and scrawled across the circle
were the words "East Side doctors!"

I understood the indignation the police felt about the
Marcus brothers. Many people were to share it, particularly when it was revealed that until some two
weeks before their death, the addicted twins had still
been on the staff of one of New York's most prestigious medical institutions, the New York Hospital–
Cornell Medical Center, and had still been treating
patients there. But it turned out that throughout their
lives, the twins had inspired indignation. In part it
was because they had always seemed to believe that,
by virtue of their twinship, they were not merely different from the rest of the world but superior to it.
One patient of theirs, a woman named Arlene Gross
who eventually gave birth to twin sons, told me that
when she was pregnant she grew very heavy, and although tests did not indicate she was carrying twins,
she thought she might be, particularly since there
was a history of twins in her family. Stewart, who was
her obstetrician, refused to consider that she might
be carrying two fetuses. "You pregnant women are all

alike," he said to her. "Just because you overeat and get fat, you think you're going to have twins." Arlene Gross continued, "And from that time on, he spoke to me with such contempt that it was as if I'd said I was going to have the Messiah, as if giving birth to twins was something too special for the likes of me."

They had been born in 1930 in Binghamton, New York, Stewart a few minutes before Cyril, and from that moment forth they led lives as intertwined as the one they had shared in their mother's womb. They were not identical, but they looked remarkably alike, and when they were toddlers spoke to one another in the secret, private language that many affect. Always together, by the time they entered school, they thought of themselves not as separate entities but, somehow, one person, albeit a person with two heads, two trunks and torsos, eight limbs, and no physical connection like that of Siamese twins. For them, the connection, the bond, was never palpable, but it existed just the same. In the first grade, the teacher asked the class members who were only children to raise their hands. Stewart and Cyril Marcus both shot up a waving, eager arm.

They were serious children, not athletic. Stewart told me once that he and Cyril almost never played ball when they were kids. Their father, a physician, bought them a chemistry set when they were little and, from an early age, playing doctor was their sport.

By the time they entered high school—their family had moved by then to Bayonne, New Jersey—their magic circle was impenetrable. They had no close friends but one another. "They didn't seem to need anyone but each other," a classmate told me. They participated in the selfsame extracurricular activities:

the student congress, the school newspaper, the school police force. They wore their hair in the same style, a high, wavy pompadour. And they dressed alike—not in the same clothes but in a style that was their own and different from that of their fellows. "It was the forties," said another classmate. "We all wore open-necked shirts and sweaters—argyle vests or those V-necked cardigans. The twins wore white shirts, ties, and jackets. They were formal all the time, as if they couldn't bear to face the world without putting on some kind of mask." Not surprisingly, when they ran for class office—Stewart for president, Cyril for treasurer—both lost.

But if they were unpopular and almost determinedly different from their fellows, they were also extraordinarily bright. Stewart won an inter–high school essay contest and, at graduation, was class valedictorian. Cyril was salutatorian. And the very fact of their being twins gave them a kind of minor celebrity at Bayonne High. They were featured in a story in the school newspaper, "Double Trouble at Bayonne High." In the story, they stressed their alikeness and said that whenever they got into mischief, their mother punished both of them in order to be sure she disciplined the right one.

The anecdote was an entertaining one, told to delight the world of singletons. But perhaps there was a grain of something other than the desire to amuse, a bona fide kernel of resentment toward their mother. Certainly years later they turned their backs on her—and indeed on anyone and anything connected to their childhood. They avoided all mention of Bayonne, with its chemical plants and crowded port. They told some patients that they came from the more elite, countrified town of Short Hills. And they communicated with their parents only on the rarest of occasions.

A woman journalist who was engaged to Stewart in the days of the twins' medical residencies believed they were not so much angry at their parents as ashamed of them. She told me that during her engagement, Stewart's parents moved from Bayonne to a suburb of New York, taking an apartment in a tall glass and concrete tower that faced the city from across the Hudson. She wanted to see her future in-laws' new place, but Stewart resisted the request for weeks. Finally, he gave in, and they drove across the river, but he was fretful and uneasy the whole way. His parents' apartment, she saw, was small and cramped, and after the visit, she was convinced that he had been reluctant to take her to see it because the modesty of the quarters embarrassed him. "The twins were snobs," she said. "I even heard that they denied to some people they knew that their parents were Jewish."

Sometimes there was humor connected with their twinship. Once, when they were interns, they participated in a hospital show, one twin exiting stage left just as his brother entered stage right, the two of them dressed alike, gesturing alike; trick photography in the flesh, it brought the house down. But increasingly the Marcus brothers struck their peers as not just distant but psychologically disturbed. "They were schizoid," said a psychiatrist who had been a medical resident with them. "When they talked to you—and most of the time they didn't talk to anyone, just to one another—you got the distinct impression that their responses were artificial, that they didn't really have the emotions that other people did, but were aping others' emotions, trying to imitate them."

"They couldn't tolerate having any experiences that weren't mutual," said a female physician who had also been a resident with them. She'd become pregnant with her first child during her residency and given birth on a night when the Marcus brothers were the gynecological residents on duty. "Having them in attendance was horrible," she told me. "One checked with his fingers to see how far I was dilated. Then he called over his brother, and had him check too. Then they did it again. It was painful enough to have one person checking the dilation, excruciating to have two people doing it. It was also, I should add, totally unnecessary. But they did it anyway. It was as if one couldn't bear to do something without sharing what he was doing with his brother."

It was during their residency that the first signs began to appear that the twins' mental disturbance was potentially dangerous. "They were arrogant, resentful of criticism, disobedient of orders," said a doctor who had been their chief resident.

The chairman of the gynecology department became concerned. He was the famous Dr. Alan Guttmacher, world-renowned specialist on family planning and himself a twin. His brother, Manfred, was a psychiatrist. Alan Guttmacher believed, and once wrote in an essay, that twins were, in a way, "monsters"—the traditional medical term for Siamese twins. They "have successfully escaped the various stages of [actual] monstrosity," he wrote, but he cautioned that unless twins worked hard at establishing separate identities, they were always in danger of turning into psychic monsters.

He must have seen that propensity for psychic

monstrosity in the Marcus twins, for one day he decided that even if they themselves would not or could not make the sanity-preserving move of separating, he would see to it that they did. He insisted they leave Mount Sinai, where they had antagonized so many people, and recommended that wherever they trained subsequently, they do so at separate institutions.

They tried to follow his advice. Stewart transferred to University Hospital at Stanford, Cyril to Joint Diseases Hospital in New York. But, after a year away, Stewart returned to New York and joined his brother at Joint Diseases.

After that year of reunion, there was a fourth year of residency still to accomplish, and Stewart went back to California. But he came back to New York as soon as the year was over, and subsequently both brothers went into private practice—a shared practice.

Still, if they were clearly intensely attached to one another, they did try to form other attachments, at least at the stage of life when their fellows were doing so. At around the time they were finishing their residencies, they each made an effort to fall in love, hoping to be married.

Stewart was the first. He began dating the journalist, who came from a well-to-do Manhattan family. After six months, they became engaged, but she began to feel that there was something mechanical about him and that he didn't truly like, let alone love, her. "He was terribly impersonal and distant," she told me. "He hardly ever introduced me to any friends. I don't think he had any. And except for an occasional kiss, he never touched me. It was the late 1950s. Sex wasn't yet what it became in the sixties, something you did without much thought. So when he didn't show any sexual drive toward me, at first I thought he was just being respectful. But when, after we got engaged, he still didn't seem to have any physical interest in me, it began to trouble me a whole lot."

Two weeks before the wedding, which was going to be held at New York's fashionable Plaza Hotel, she called off the ceremony. "I finally realized there was something terribly wrong with Stewart and that I shouldn't just go ahead and marry him. The night I decided this, I tried to tell him, but he was so into his own mind, he didn't even seem to hear me at first. I had to pull the engagement ring he'd given me off my finger and stuff it into his pocket to get his attention, and once I had his attention, he turned furious. How could I do this when people had already bought wedding gifts? he kept saying, as if that were more important than my feelings, our futures."

Stewart's onetime fiancée remembered further that both the twins frequently made inappropriate remarks, recalling, "Cyril once asked my mother outright just how much money and property Stewart could expect if he married me. My mother was horrified. And Stewart, who had a very high opinion of himself and his brother, but of almost no one else, was always correcting and criticizing other people. Once he got violently mad at me because I said something about the airline, Pan Am. What was wrong? I asked him. He said I was being ungrammatical, and shouted, 'There's no such airline as Pan Am. It's Pan *American!*'"

She was relieved when she finally ended the engagement. "I never felt at all sentimental or nostalgic afterward," she said. "You know the way music, say, or flowers can make you remember something from the past? I felt none of that. Stewart had been so impersonal that in a way it was as if I had never known him."

Why had she wanted to marry him? I asked at one point.

"Those were the days when a girl was *supposed* to grow up and try to catch herself a doctor," she said bluntly.

Stewart was never to marry. But shortly after his aborted engagement, Cyril did.

It was a relatively short-lived event. In 1969, after nine years of marriage and two daughters, his wife asked for a divorce. He was too perfectionistic, she complained to friends. He was explosive and irrational. And he had no respect for anyone but his brother.

The two of them were together all the time after that. Cyril took the apartment on York Avenue, in the same building in which Stewart lived. Then he and Stewart took to traveling together on vacations, sharing a summer house in the Hamptons, dining *à deux* in chic Manhattan restaurants. And they never again attempted to include a third person in their tight, mutually circling orbit.

Perhaps, had they not been so close, they might have conquered the aloofness that coursed through their bodies like a numbing anesthetic through bodily tissues. Some schizoid individuals who have no one with whom to share their hours occasionally do. But because the brothers had one another, they turned only to one another. They viewed their bond as sustaining and nourishing. But it was, in fact, a disease that would eventually kill them.

* * *

Their medical practice was flourishing in the sixties, for the Marcuses were among the few surgeons then to have perfected the "purse string," an operation that enabled women whose wombs were unable to bear the weight of a developing fetus to carry their babies to full term. They did research into infertility and published numerous scientific papers suggesting new treatments for the barren. They co-authored a textbook, *Advances in Obstetrics and Gynecology*, that was considered a classic in the field. They received hospital privileges at both Lenox Hill and New York hospitals, and the latter made them faculty members of its medical school. Successful and well connected, they inspired the confidence of colleagues, who gave them numerous referrals.

But they were, almost invariably, irascible and prone to irrational outbursts. A patient who was pregnant for the first time late in life, when the risk of having a retarded child is greatest, told me that she asked Cyril to arrange to give her infant a PKU test, a test for mental retardation now required by law and automatically received by all infants born in New York State. The test was not, however, standard procedure at that time, and Cyril flew off the handle at her request. She was being demanding, he told her. She was being pathologically anxious. Why, he hadn't even had the test done for his own children. Then, shortly before her child was born, the test became law. The patient felt that Cyril would now see that she had been right to request it, but if anything he became even more angry with her. "He hated to be wrong about anything," she said.

Another woman had a similar experience with Stewart. She inquired whether a certain medication he had prescribed for her was safe to use during pregnancy, and he—no doubt feeling that his judgment had been called into question—became defensive, shouted at her, and threatened to throw her out of his office.

These were not isolated incidents. Over time, I heard accounts like this from dozens of women who had used the Marcus brothers as their obstetrician-gynecologists.

But if the brothers were always explosive and paranoid, they became even more so once Cyril separated from his wife and he and his twin began relying solely on one another for companionship. A nurse who quit their employ after working for them throughout the late 1960s said of Cyril, "He would sit down and you would see an expression on his face change, and all of a sudden he would become a totally different person—arrogant, nasty, biting, cutting."

So extreme were his tantrums that one day he threw a sterilizer full of instruments at her. She quit, never to return.

No one knows whether all along, from the days of their medical school training, the twins were taking drugs. No one knows whether their tendency to be quarrelsome and to explode into tantrums was natural, an artifact of their personalities, or a chemically induced phenomenon. But certainly by the early 1970s both of the Marcus brothers—still delivering babies, still performing operations—were addicted to several substances, among them amphetamines and barbiturates. Druggists' records indicate that they repeatedly ordered these drugs for themselves, making out their prescription forms to nonexistent patients.

In 1972, Cyril seems to have taken an overdose of

some drug or another. That summer, the handyman in his building, an expansive fellow named Bill Terrell, was passing Cyril's apartment on his way from a repair job on the floor when he heard a buzzing noise within. It sounded like a telephone off the hook. Terrell thought nothing of it until, several hours later, he was again on Cyril's floor and again heard the buzzing. This time he rang Cyril's doorbell and, when he got no answer, began to pound on the door.

No one responded. Terrell went downstairs and telephoned Stewart immediately. "There's something not quite kosher at your brother's place," he told him. "I think he needs your help."

What happened next amazed and intrigued Terrell. There was a long silence. Then Stewart put the phone down. The handyman hung on, but Stewart didn't get back on the phone for a long while. Terrell had the feeling that he was somehow consulting the air waves, communing with his brother. Other people have speculated that Stewart was considering letting his brother die so that he might at long last escape from the monstrosity of being a double. But most likely he was simply trying to pull himself together, to mobilize himself out of some drugged condition of his own. Whatever the reason, it was a good minute and a half before he got back on the phone and at last said, "You're right. He needs help. I'll be right over."

Still, once he arrived on Cyril's floor, Stewart seemed oddly lethargic and slow to grasp what needed to be done. The door was locked from the inside, and Terrell had to insist that they break into the apartment. When they did, they saw Cyril lying fully dressed and unconscious in the foyer of the apartment. Stewart turned pale and said, "He's dead," then stood there passively. Terrell was the one to put his ear to Cyril's chest and say "He's not dead. He's still breathing."

"Give him artificial respiration," Stewart then directed.

"You're the doctor," Terrell said. "You do it."

"I can't," Stewart replied. And he stood stock still, unable to move.

In the end, Terrell yelled for help, and some other doctors who lived in the building arrived and gave Cyril mouth-to-mouth resuscitation and called an ambulance for him.

He was hospitalized briefly. But soon he was back in the office, seeing patients.

In the next few years, the physical condition of both brothers deteriorated and their emotional control evaporated. Stubborn to the point of self-destructiveness, they were now refusing to fill out medical insurance forms for their patients, saying the activity wasted their time, and they would engage in screaming arguments with patients who badgered them about the forms. Cyril, angry at a hospitalized patient who complained that an intravenous needle was badly inserted and was hurting her, grabbed the bottle of intravenous liquid and hurled it onto the floor. Stewart, under contract to edit a second volume about advances in obstetrics and gynecology, lost the manuscripts of fellow doctors whose research articles were to have been in the book and spoke so antagonistically to his publisher that he decided to drop the project. The twins' office grew dirty, disarrayed. The rent went unpaid. The air conditioner broke down and was never repaired. And their nurses would frequently receive calls from them in which, in slurred voices, they would direct the nurses to cancel their day's appointments.

* * *

It will forever be a stain on the history of medicine in America that the Marcus twins, whose psychological condition was known to their colleagues—if not fully recognized as a drug problem—were allowed to continue to practice and to remain on the staff of a major New York hospital. But they were. And although the hospital did eventually drop them, the decision was not made in time to prevent the brothers from jeopardizing the safety of several patients.

In March 1974, Cyril, sweating profusely and unsteady on his feet, undertook to circumcise a newborn infant. A technician who was in the room with him looked up to see that his hands were shaking and that he was trying to cut the baby's foreskin by sawing it with the dull handle of his surgical instrument. Terrified, she ran for help. But when the help she had summoned—several other doctors, including the head of the department—arrived, Cyril was allowed, under their supervision, to complete the procedure.

A year later, in March of 1975, a similar incident occurred, but this time it was Stewart who, pale, weak, and with unsteady hands, undertook a circumcision. This time it was a nurse who intervened, and this time Stewart was enjoined from continuing the procedure and sent home.

Between these two incidents, the chairman of New York Hospital's Department of Obstetrics and Gynecology did make an effort to restrict the activities of the brothers. Cyril, who one day collapsed outside an operating room and hurt his head so badly that he required hospitalization, was instructed to take a four-month medical leave of absence. And Stewart was asked to take a vacation, which he did—for a month. But even in the period that the brothers were theoretically personas non grata at the hospital, they somehow managed to continue to admit patients.

Why would patients continue to use them, continue visiting their intolerably dirty office, bearing their infuriating taunts and tantrums? In a way, this was the greatest mystery of all about the Marcus brothers' case—or a tragic fact about women as consumers of medicine. Several of the women I spoke with who had remained patients of the twins until the bitter end explained to me that when the doctors flew off the handle, they'd assumed they themselves were somehow at fault, thus they'd accepted whatever rage was directed at them. Others told me that the opposite side of the brothers' rages was reminiscence and revelation: with their waiting room no longer full, as it had been in the sixties, the doctors would often spend hours with their remaining patients, talking about their philosophy of life, their fear of death, their conviction that "the good die, the bad live on," and they felt flattered by these attentions.

Susan S. Lichtendorf, a woman whose first child was delivered by Caesarean section by Stewart Marcus only weeks before the twins died, wrote an article in *Ms.* magazine in which she explained the insecurity and respect for medical authority that kept her seeing the Marcuses despite their obvious peculiarities: "I didn't want to seem...like a 'difficult" pregnant woman by questioning my doctors, so I overlooked the fact that they kept forgetting to make my hospital reservation." And, "I squelched suspicion....I was glad that in a city famous for money-mad doctors who jam their waiting rooms and whiz through examining rooms, the Marcus twins appeared to be limiting their practice and took time with me."

Why their hospital tolerated them is another matter. It may have been because their supervisors and colleagues, remembering their past accomplishments, felt a certain loyalty to them and cherished the hope that in time they would be rehabilitated. But more likely it was because, as several doctors have suggested, the machinery for dismissing a doctor is extremely cumbersome. Unless a hospital can *prove* that a doctor deserves to be dismissed, he can level a mighty lawsuit against his institution.

Nevertheless, by 1975 Dr. Fritz Fuchs, chairman of obstetrics and gynecology, seems to have at last decided to try to prove such an argument. Probably hoping to arm himself with sufficient evidence that the twins were addicted to drugs, he asked the other members of his staff, doctors and nurses alike, to keep the Marcus brothers under careful scrutiny and to alert him whenever they admitted a patient. He did not know at that time that they had already been dismissed—Cyril in 1973, Stewart in 1974—by Lenox Hill. But he did know that as a result of complaints from patients whose insurance forms hadn't been filed, the twins were being investigated by the New York County Medical Society.

Fuchs' staff watched the brothers closely, and one day in the spring of 1975 the chairman informed them that they were under suspicion of being drug addicts. Unless they did something about their habit, he warned them, New York Hospital would soon dismiss them.

They denied that they were addicts.

Fuchs repeated the charge, and offered them two choices. They could either take a medical leave of absence, and get treatment for the drug problem, or they could resign.

They were enraged. They argued with him. They pointed out that whichever course they took, they would lose their reputations.

The chairman was unmoved and repeated that they must get treatment or resign. If they did not, when their current appointment at the hospital expired on June 30, they would not be reappointed. He gave them until June 12 to let him know which path they would be choosing.

They didn't get back to him, and on June 12 he called them, reaching Stewart. Stewart said they'd been unable to decide what to do and asked for more time. He'd call the chairman with their decision by June 16, he promised.

He never did, and the next day Fuchs recommended to the hospital's board that the twins be dropped.

It was, unfortunately, a decision that was not made in time to prevent a near calamity. On June 17, one of the Marcus brothers' pregnant patients arrived at the hospital's emergency room bleeding severely and apparently aborting. Cyril admitted her, then left the hospital. She continued to bleed profusely. Three hours later, Stewart arrived. According to the woman's husband, who had been waiting all this time for someone to staunch his wife's hemorrhaging, Stewart was sweating, barely coherent, and "looked like a drunk who was just pulled to his feet and about to fall over again." When he examined the patient, he seemed not even to notice that she was bleeding and directed the distraught husband to take her home.

The husband sought assistance. Other physicians assumed control of the patient. Stewart was directed to leave the premises. And that day was his and Cyril's last at the hospital.

In the next few weeks, the brothers finally attempted to right their self-destructive course. Although they were callous men, reckless, self-centered, and irresponsible, one must in the end feel some pity for them, for they made a risky, dangerous stab at change. They holed up in Cyril's apartment, laid in a stock of food, drink, and anticonvulsive medication, and tried, on their own and without assistance, to withdraw from barbiturates.

They must have suffered, even felt seizures coming on, for they consumed the anticonvulsant. Then they must have lost their will for withdrawal, for they went out and obtained barbiturates. Bottles of Nembutal with late June drugstore dates were found in the apartment—empty.

After this, they remained in the rooms together, speaking to no one, letting the phone ring unanswered, rarely eating, barely conscious, so drugged that one of them, at least, could not maneuver his way to the toilet and made use of the armchair.

On July 10, New York Hospital's medical board met and discussed dropping the twins from the staff. And sometime between July 10 and July 14, Stewart took an overdose of Nembutal and died.

Cyril was still alive, and perhaps for a moment he considered saving himself. He left the apartment, took the elevator down to the lobby, and started to make his way out of the building and into the world. He was observed by the doorman, who, noticing how sick he looked, offered to help him negotiate his passage.

Cyril dismissed the doorman's solicitude with astonishing rudeness and sudden strength. "I can manage on my own," he said, brushing him away. But of course he couldn't. He and Stewart had spent too many years managing as one person. After shrugging off the doorman, he abruptly returned to his apartment. Perhaps he had realized that, alive, he would forever be—like most other people in the world—an isolated, separate being, and the thought was odious to him.

Inside, he did all the things that suicides usually do. He left a kind of note, typing the name and address of his former wife on a piece of paper and tucking it into his typewriter. He even tried to leave a clue about his decision to die with Stewart. He placed a copy of Iris Murdoch's novel *A Fairly Honorable Defeat* face down on a pile of papers in the middle of one of the rooms. The story of a cynical man who tries to break up the love affair between a homosexual and his lover, but succeeds in causing, instead, the suicide of the homosexual's elder brother, it is a book about separation and loss; it was the only book found lying about in Cyril's apartment. His other books, chiefly scientific works, were all neatly shelved when police entered the otherwise chaotic rooms.

After setting out the note and the book, Cyril seems simply to have sat still. Apparently he took no further drugs, for the autopsy revealed none in his system. And apparently, again according to the autopsy, he did not experience a seizure. He seems, rather, to have died as a result of remaining at Stewart's side for several days, eating nothing and growing ever more emaciated, waiting for death to come and reunite him with his twin.

A day or two later, neighbors complained of a smell

emanating from the apartment. "They thought there was a dead rat or something in there," handyman Bill Terrell said.

He went to the door of the apartment—and then, without entering, summoned the police. "I knew at once what that smell meant," he said. "I'd been in combat."

Many people I spoke with after the twins died felt that there was something mystical about Cyril's behavior and suggested that he had been, in effect, almost drawn against his will to share his brother's fate. It made me realize that some primitive terror of twins still lurks in contemporary man. We have come eons away from the kinds of superstition that drove the aborigines of Australia to murder one or even both of a twin set at birth, that prompted some West African tribes to kill not just twin infants but the women who had given birth to them. But some of us (perhaps like the Marcus brothers themselves) nevertheless attribute to twins superhuman sensitivities like extrasensory perception or the ability to communicate without words. And when these doubles, born on the same day, die at the same time, their fate arouses in us an almost primordial anxiety.

How can it happen? It can't, and yet it does. It happened in New York in 1952 when two ancient twin sisters were found withered from malnutrition in a Greenwich Village apartment, only to expire after their discovery within hours of each other. It happened in North Carolina in 1962 when twin brothers, hospitalized for schizophrenia, were found dead within minutes of each other at separate ends of the institution. The simultaneous or nearly simultaneous death of twins happens rarely, but when it does, it seems like some mysterious arithmetical proposition far beyond the ordinary computation involved in life and death, and it so frightens and unnerves us that we seek extrarational explanations.

But mysticism is unnecessary in the case of the Marcus brothers. The explanation for their nearly simultaneous deaths lies in the extraordinary attachment they felt toward one another and the extraordinary disregard they felt for the world of singletons.

THE DOWNWARD DRIFT OF A HIGH SCHOOL STAR

Torrington, Connecticut, and
New York, New York

1981

I became interested in the case of Gerard Coury, a young man from Connecticut who met his death in a New York City subway station, because there was something about the story that did not jell. Coury had been set upon by a gang of Forty-second Street regulars—pushers and panhandlers, the addicted and the addled—sometime in the red-eye hours of a summer Saturday in 1981. Shirtless when they surrounded him, he emerged from the crowd's midst altogether naked. Then, in a state of panic, he began running down the street. The mob followed, jeering and pelting him with beer cans. Two transit police officers attempted to intercede, but Coury bolted from them, too. Racing, he ran into a Times Square subway station, leaped onto the tracks, touched the third rail twice, and died.

Many things about the story, at least as reported in the newspapers, were puzzling. For one thing, Coury had not, as might have been expected, died of electrocution but rather—according to the medical examiner, who found no burn marks on the body—because his heart had stopped. Further, it was reported that someone in the crowd told a transit officer that the mob had stripped Coury of his trousers. But it was also reported that detectives were unable to find anyone who'd actually witnessed the stripping. Additionally, several New York police officers said they'd seen Coury, shoeless and shirtless, dazedly talking to himself, earlier in the day. One officer, a transit policeman in Grand Central Terminal, told reporters he'd even detained and questioned Coury, who said that he'd lost his clothes and all his money in a mugging that had occurred a week or two earlier and that he'd been trying to get home ever since. But Coury's parents said that the young man had been home just three days before.

There was more that was perplexing. The transit officer who had detained Coury in the station had suggested that since he had no money for a ticket home, he call his family and ask someone to fetch him or get money to him. Coury in fact telephoned his parents in Connecticut, and soon afterward the police received a call from someone who said he was the young man's uncle and that he'd be down shortly to take him home. Coury said he'd be in the waiting room. But later the uncle called the police and said he couldn't come. The police went to give the young man this latest news, but they couldn't find him. He wasn't in the waiting room or, for that matter, anywhere in the station. Apparently, like someone with little grasp on reality, he'd wandered away without waiting for his anticipated rescuer. Yet, according to his parents, the young man had "no mental problems."

None of the pieces of the story quite came together to make a comprehensible whole. Nevertheless, what had happened to Coury quickly came to be viewed as a sorry symbol of the inhumanity of New York, a Kitty Genovese case for the eighties. Several newspapers said Coury had been "frightened to death." A national magazine, headlining its report NAKED VIOLENCE IN NEW YORK and terming Coury the "straight-arrow son of a middle-class family," implied that the young man had been a kind of Everyman, Mr. Small Town America, an average citizen who met his death simply because of the callousness and cruelty of a big-city crowd. Soon, people everywhere began saying that but for the grace of God, what had happened to Coury on the streets of New York could have happened to you or me.

I didn't believe it. I simply couldn't rid myself of the impression that there was something odd about the incident. It just didn't seem feasible to me that an ordinary citizen, pursued by a terrifying crowd, would have fled when police tried to help him. I began to feel certain that if I looked beneath the surface, I would discover that in some way Coury had been complicit in his own death.

Perhaps I wanted to discover this because, as psychiatrists who study the new field of "victimology" are always quick to point out, all of us like to believe that there are no *innocent* victims. If a victim can be found to have provoked or somehow contributed to his own destruction, then the rest of us can—theoretically, at least—learn to eschew the kind of behavior that did in the unfortunate fellow, and thus we can feel, somehow, safe. Safer, anyway. Of course, I *know* there are innocent victims. There are children playing on streetcorners who get shot by cruising snipers. Women are raped and beaten by strangers, men robbed and mutilated by macho marauders they have never before laid eyes on. Nevertheless, I couldn't quite swallow that Coury's ordeal had occurred simply because he'd been in the wrong place at the wrong time. It's *such* a wrong place—Times Square, at least at that time—the middle of the night. Why had Coury been there? And what sort of man had he been?

I began by getting in touch with his mother, Mary Coury, an articulate, maternal-sounding woman who had been devastated by the loss of her son but who nevertheless agreed to talk with me. She said it was because she wanted the world to know the kind of family Gerry had come from. It was a family that hailed from Torrington, Connecticut, a quiet town in the northwestern corner of the state. There, Mary Coury, and her husband, Nimar, a Lebanese American, had settled down more than forty years earlier. And there they'd raised seven children, six boys and a girl. Gerard had been the youngest. He was twenty-six years old when he died.

Mary Coury was proud of her family. "All our kids went to college," was the first thing she pointed out to me. "My husband is a factory worker, and I never went further than high school, but we sent all our kids to college."

It was easy to understand her pride. The Courys had often been hard pressed to make ends meet. But Nimar Coury had augmented his factory wages by servicing candy vending machines, and Mary had been an astute household manager. Somehow, the couple had begun to live out the American dream: to arrange for their children to have a better life than they had had. "All our children have done well," Mary Coury said. "And their children will do even better."

The eldest son, David, attended West Point and served in the U.S. Army until his retirement a few years before. Marcia, the only daughter, graduated from the University of Hartford and eventually entered the computer division of a large insurance company. ("She was one of the first people the company ever trained for computer work," Mrs. Coury told me proudly.) The next child, John, went to Boston College, then on to American University for an M.A., and took a job with the Agency for International Development in Panama. Another son, Bill, went to Niagara College and then into business on the island of Barbados. Nimar Jr. had two years at Allegheny College, in Pennsylvania, on a scholarship. And Charles, the next son, had attended the University of Connecticut and was working at a school for troubled adolescents in nearby Litchfield.

"Gerry may have been the brightest of the bunch," said his mother. "He had a ninety-one average in high school and was a member of the National Honor Society."

I was to hear a similar account of Gerry Coury by talking with his high school principal, Marvin Maskovsky, a sincere, friendly man. He told me that Gerry hadn't been *just* bright. In his halcyon days, he had been one of those rare, well-rounded boys, the kind who excel at both sports and studies. He was a center on the Torrington High football team for four years and manager of the baseball and basketball teams for two. Scholastically, he'd ranked forty-fifth in his class of 390. He'd been voted "hardest worker" and "most influential" by his classmates; he'd been president of the Key Club, a junior branch of the Kiwanis Club; and he'd been a school leader, the kind of boy, said Maskovsky, "to whom a teacher could go to discuss a class problem, and who could be counted upon to give sound advice and cooperation."

Maskovsky had a detailed example of what a cooperative young man Gerry had been. He remembered that the first year he was principal, he'd gotten "this idea that it might give our graduation ceremony a certain loftiness and importance if the kids gave some kind of ovation to the faculty. But it was a question in my mind, because you're never sure how kids are going to feel about that sort of thing. So I called Gerry Coury into my office. I asked him what he thought of the idea. And Gerry went away and thought about it and talked it over with the other seniors, and he came back and said, 'Yes, it's a great idea,' and the students did it, and it was very moving. That was the kind of boy Gerry was. He was my emissary to the other kids."

Maskovsky sounded truly sad. He went on to tell me that ever since Gerry's death, he'd been thinking about him and leafing through the pages of his yearbook, the 1973 *Torringtonian*. There was Gerry, in portrait after portrait, group shot after group shot, always neatly dressed, vibrant, clear-eyed. "He was a star," the principal said.

I thought briefly, after talking with Maskovsky, that perhaps I'd been wrong about Coury. Perhaps, after all, he *had* been a straight-arrow sort of fellow. But a call to the New York Police Department sent me back to my original theory. They too had a photograph of Coury, they said. A picture taken by a police photographer just after his death. In their picture, Gerry was dirty, unkempt, deteriorated. "Like a derelict," one police officer told me, his voice hushed. "And it isn't as if he looks like he'd just gotten that way overnight, or because of what happened to him right before. He had several days' growth of beard, and his body was filthy. He looked as if he'd been this way a long time."

And another policeman, one of the several who'd noticed Coury *before* he died, described him as "smelly."

More intrigued than ever, I decided to make a trip to Torrington to try to unravel the story.

On a fiercely hot day in July 1981, I drove the hundred miles from New York to Torrington. Happily, the town (population 31,000), is nestled in the foothills of the Berkshires, so it was about ten degrees cooler than New York. Indeed, it seemed, as I drove through its center, like a green and pristine paradise: tree-lined streets, a lushly planted village green called Coe Memorial Park, old Victorian houses, tall-steepled churches. The New England town of everybody's fantasy. But within minutes of my arrival I was forced to consider that nowadays, even pretty, rural towns have big-city problems. Driving down a broad, uncongested avenue, I suddenly heard a brazening of sirens, and when I pulled to the side, I learned from a shaken bystander that a bank had just been robbed, the robbers had made a stunning getaway, and the police were in pursuit. Before the day was out, I was to experience even more vividly how alike small towns and big cities are today.

I went first to look at the street where Coury had grown up. It was right in town, but it was nothing like the streets I'd passed through earlier. The Coury home was on a partly industrial block in a neglected, decaying neighborhood. Porches sagged, windows were broken, and houses were in sore need of paint. This was another Torrington, a place of doldrums and despair.

The Torrington doldrums cannot be overlooked in the story of Gerry Coury. At the turn of the century, when river power was still important, Torrington was a thriving industrial city, producing brass, copper, and metalware. The town absorbed waves of immigrants —chiefly Italians, Irish, and like the Courys, Lebanese—who thrived in the New England setting. But in recent decades, Torrington had fallen upon bleak times. Old industries had shut down, and new ones had been slow to replace them. In 1981, the average weekly wage, $238, was among the lowest of any Connecticut city. Unemployment that year was so high that Torrington was one of only fifteen Connecticut cities promised special consideration on federal government contracts. Because of the low wages and high unemployment, the ambitious young had tended to leave Torrington, which left the town with a disproportionate number of old people.

For the young who did not leave, there wasn't much to do. On Main Street, the formerly elegant, much-frequented movie house had closed. So, too, had quite a few of the clothing stores and coffee shops. And in Gerry Coury's neighborhood, the closet thing to a lively gathering place was a shabby, drearily lighted all-night diner.

No one was at the Coury house that morning, so I started driving around the area to try to interview some of the people who'd known Gerry. There was Father Joseph Amar, pastor of St. Maron's Church, around the corner from the Courys'. Father Amar said that Gerry had been very active in church affairs when he was an adolescent but that in recent years he hadn't seen much of him because Coury had "apparently fallen on hard times." There was Eddie Barber, manager of the Moosehead Tavern, a bar that Gerry used to frequent. Barber said that Gerry "had his strange ways. Sometimes he'd walk in with his

head hanging down and just not talk to anybody."
There was a friend of Gerry's who didn't want to be
identified, who told me that Gerry had changed since
high school, saying, "He got kind of strange, with-
drew into himself. He became a loner, and he got
kind of down on everything, saying the guys with big
money ran the whole show."

These observations were corroborated by Owen
Quinn, a schoolmate of Gerry's who had become the
director of Torrington's social services. In his professional capacity, he'd seen quite a bit of Gerry in recent
years. He said Gerry was "cynical" and saw the world
as a "dog-eat-dog place." "Like when Tai Babilonia
and Randy Gardner had to withdraw from the Olym-
pics," Quinn tried to explain. "You know, most people
were sad and disappointed. But Gerry said, 'I'm glad.
I'm glad they can't compete. This country is always
making heroes over nothing.' Gerry used to be a very
outgoing, optimistic sort of guy. But he got very distant and sort of depressed in the last two or three
years."

I began to realize that the Gerry Coury whom his
mother and his principal had spoken about was not
the only Gerry Coury. That perhaps theirs was a Gerry
Coury who had ceased to exist long before a man
with the same name and features met his death in
the New York subway station. Gerry Coury had
changed.

It didn't take me very long to find out why. A visit
to the local newspaper office produced an important
item of information that had been left out of all publi-
cations except those in Torrington and nearby towns.
Coury, the town police had told the newspaper, had
been part of the local "drug culture." The New York
newspapers and the national magazine that had

painted Gerry Coury as a "straight-arrow" youth hadn't reported this. They'd either neglected to call the Connecticut press and police or—perhaps because it made a better, a more chilling, story to portray Coury as an innocent, a mere passer-by on that Main Street of the nation's drug business, Forty-second Street—they'd obtained but chosen to ignore the information.

The center of the drug culture in Torrington was the lovely village green I'd seen when I first entered the town, Coe Memorial Park. I also found out that, just as in New York, the culture was composed chiefly of young men who led aimless, rootless lives. Gerry had apparently been part of this alienated group for some time. But in the weeks before his death his life became particularly rootless. He not only had no job and no girlfriend, but he had no home. For a time, he'd shared a house with friends, but in the middle of June they'd kicked him out. After that, he spent his days in the park. At night, he bedded down in a parked car.

It was difficult to pin down exactly when the honor student's descent started, but it must have been sometime in his early college years. After his graduation from Torrington High, Gerry had gone off to Fairfield University in Fairfield County, Connecticut. There, things began to go wrong. A dean told me Gerry showed signs, while at Fairfield, of being very "disturbed." He'd become involved—"overinvolved," said the dean—with the remnants of the campus counterculture of the 1960s and early 1970s. He kept demanding "relevant" courses and kept tangling with the administration. At the end of his third year, Gerry dropped out of Fairfield, and the university advised his family that he needed psychological counseling.

Sadly, either the family did not or Coury would not accept this advice. The young man simply came back to Torrington and, with few opportunities for either employment or entertainment, began to deteriorate. He did find work occasionally—once as a waiter at the Kilravock Inn in Litchfield, a famous old hotel that caught fire the summer Gerry worked there. ("It burned down the week he left," Mrs. Coury told me. "We always kidded him that he must have burned the place down.") He pumped gas for a while and worked as a security guard. But eventually he always failed. He lost his security guard job because, said his mother, "he fell asleep one night, or came to work late. Something like that."

When he wasn't working, Coury would just drift. He traveled to New Jersey. To New York. To Florida. Even to California. How he got the money for his trips, no one seemed to know. But now Gerry was drifting both across America and downward.

There is in psychiatry a fundamental concept called the downward-drift hypothesis. Psychiatrists use it to explain why, when most individuals in America's still-expanding economy and still-fluid class structure invariably seem to progress, both economically and socially, beyond the levels of their parents, certain people not only do not exceed their parents but drop to progressively lower and lower strata of society. Such individuals, goes the theory, spiral downward in class because they suffer from psychiatric disorders—schizophrenia, alcoholism, drug abuse. From all I had learned in Torrington, it was clear that Gerry Coury exemplified the downward-drift hypothesis. He'd failed to live up to his siblings' achievements and to his parents' aspirations because he had had the psychiatric disorder of drug abuse.

To gain some insight into the sort of life Gerry had ultimately led, I went over to Coe Memorial Park and hung around for a while. I wasn't frightened, even though quite a few of the benches near me were filled with scruffy, unkempt youths who seemed stoned. Perhaps it was because, as a city-dweller, I still couldn't rid myself of the notion that anything that looked as idyllic as this verdant park simply couldn't be dangerous, no matter its denizens. Or perhaps it was because I'd been told that ever since the Coury story had broken, the Torrington police were keeping a close eye on the park.

Whatever the reason, I sat in the park and quietly observed my neighbors. They were, for the most part, barefoot and wearing nothing but jeans—just the way Gerry had been dressed, wandering about midtown Manhattan. After a while, I began to strike up a conversation with some of the young men. Had they known Gerry Coury? I wanted to know.

It turned out that quite a few of them had, and soon we were talking. Yes, Gerry had hung out here a lot, they told me. Yes, for the most part they'd liked him. "He was real mellow," one young man said. But another, a gaunt, sad-eyed man, interrupted, "Except when he got funny."

"What do you mean, funny?" I asked.

"Paranoid. When he got high, he'd get paranoid. He'd shout and scream."

Then the man began to nod and smile to himself. He shut his pained-looking eyes and began to look happier, and faraway. It was as if I suddenly wasn't there, as if no one was there, and he was alone with his daydreams. I tried to bring him back to reality by asking him some more questions. But I think he truly didn't hear me. He began laughing and cackling.

That night as I drove home I began to understand what had happened to Coury in New York City—and why the tale had seemed so mysterious. Coury hadn't lost his shoes and shirt in a mugging. He'd just been wandering around the city in the same garb he and his Torrington cronies were accustomed to wearing. He hadn't waited in Grand Central for his parents to send someone to "rescue" him, perhaps because he knew that after years of his erratic behavior they wouldn't do so, or perhaps simply because he was just too stoned to remember to wait. And as to the Forty-second Street crowd's having stripped him of his trousers and subsequently taunted him, it seemed just as likely that he himself, deep in some dazed, drug-induced daydream of his own, had begun to take off his own pants, thereby arousing the crowd's jeering.

No drug traces were found in Coury's body. But there are some drugs, notably LSD, that are difficult to detect. From Coury's behavior earlier in the day— the confused laughing and talking to himself that police who'd seen him in Midtown and at Grand Central had reported—it seemed plausible indeed that he'd taken, or perhaps unknowingly been given, some sort of a hallucinogen such as LSD. A bad trip on a hallucinogen would have made him frightened of everyone—not just of the crowd, but of the police who tried to help him. A bad trip would have enmeshed him thoroughly in a monstrous private nightmare.

Certainly, observers who'd seen Coury in the last

few minutes of his life had seen a man lost in a nightmare. "He was just bugged out," a thirteen-year-old Forty-second Street hanger-on said. "He never spoke," said the transit officer who'd tried to protect him from the jeering crowd behind him. "He never said a word! We tried to hold him, but he pulled away and ducked into the subway."

I felt sure, as I reached the city, that Coury had not so much been frightened to death by the crowd as that he'd been frightened to death by a drug overdose. For witness the precise details of that death: he touched the third rail *twice*; after touching it the first time, he flipped backward, took six deep breaths, reached over, and touched it again. Most likely, he'd been so thoroughly, so inutterably panicked that he could imagine no help, no relief from his terror, save the relief of death.

Why had the story in the papers and the national magazine seemed so bewildering? Well, the reporters hadn't used any information about Coury that came from the Torrington police or press. They'd relied on his mother. And she, as mothers will, had offered a glowing picture of her son. It was easy, now that he was dead. So, denying his problems to the world at large, possibly even denying them to herself, she'd gone ahead and painted him, not as the man he had become, but as the boy, the high school star, he'd once been.

That was the end of the puzzle, but for me it was the beginning of a period of anger. I was indignant at all the people who were blaming New York for what had happened to Coury.

There were many such people. One of them, a Tor-rington friend of Coury's, wrote a letter to the *New*

York Times in which he raged against the "mob of underdogs" who'd run after Gerry, "those nameless punks who live on trash and broken homes." The letterwriter spoke of being disillusioned, of having once cared and worried about the "disadvantaged," but of having become convinced, as a result of what happened to Gerry, that the disadvantaged should be "kept away, at almost any cost," from the rest of society. "I want government, which is charged with our general welfare, to step in, with Federal Troops if necessary, and protect my life as I walk the streets of America's cities," he wrote. Big cities was what he meant. "I have three brothers who live in big cities, and I don't want to lose any of them."

I felt that what had happened to Coury wasn't a New York tragedy or even a big-city tragedy. It was an American tragedy. All over the country, hundreds of thousands of youths were suffering from the disorder that had afflicted Gerry Coury. There is an epidemic of downward drifters in America, I kept thinking, and Forth-second Street is only one gathering place for these restless souls. There are also—I couldn't put it out of my mind—Coe Memorial Parks in innumerable American towns.

A TRAGEDY ON EIGHTY-NINTH STREET

New York, New York

1980

On a September Saturday when summer vacation was drawing to a close and the school term just about to begin, a thirty-four-year-old New Yorker named Irene Schwartz drove her two children out to the Great Adventure amusement park, in New Jersey. On Sunday, she took them to Central Park. On Monday and Tuesday, she made preparations for their return to their classrooms, scheduling a dentist's appointment for seven-year-old Joshua and a nursery teacher's home visit for five-year-old Judy. Then, sometime on Tuesday, she left her co-op on East Eighty-ninth Street in Manhattan, drove out to Farmingdale, Long Island, and purchased a shotgun. That night, or early Wednesday morning, she went into the bedrooms where Joshua and Judy lay sleeping, shot them in the head, carried their lifeless bodies into her own bedroom, lay down between them on her big bed, and shot herself.

Why? The mind recoils, the imagination stumbles, particularly since Irene Schwartz had been a well-educated, well-off, and, above all, *motherly* woman.

Her friends and neighbors were numb with disbelief. One said to me, "One of the most awful things about what happened is that it makes you feel that if a woman like *that* could kill her kids, then none of us is safe. It could happen to anyone. You see, she seemed to have all the pieces of her life in place. There just weren't any warning signs." Another said, "I used to watch her as she went about her chores and think to myself, *God, I wish I could be more like her.* Now I feel not just sad but scared." And a third said, "She was so loving. If she did something like this, could I? Could I flip right out one day when I'm stuck home with the kids and they're screaming and my husband's away and school hasn't started yet? Could I just up and shoot them?"

To these women, what happened to Irene Schwartz appeared so incomprehensible that it brought them not only sorrow but terror—the terror that always explodes when life seems arbitrary and one can fathom no cause and effect in the universe. It was largely to still this terror, to explain that there was some cause and effect in the story of Irene Schwartz, that I undertook writing about her.

"We tell ourselves stories in order to live," Joan Didion wrote in *The White Album*. "We look for the sermon in the suicide, for the moral or social lesson in the murder of five. . . . We live entirely, especially if we are writers, by the imposition of a narrative line upon disparate images, by the 'ideas' with which we have learned to freeze the shifting phantasmagoria which is our actual experience."

In the case of Irene Schwartz, there was no moral or social lesson to satisfy our need to find patterns in the world and thus feel safe. But there was a psychiatric lesson. There *were* warning signs, however Irene Schwartz's life may have looked to the outside world.

* * *

Certainly her life appeared temperate, comfortable, even enviable. Irene and her husband, forty-three-year-old Robert Schwartz, a professor of economics at New York University's Graduate School of Business Administration, lived in one of Manhattan's most fashionable, most placid neighborhoods, the East Eighties, just off Park Avenue. There they had, as Irene's father, Alfred Schwarzchild, president of the Royal Mills textile firm, told me, "no financial worries. None at all." Their valuable co-op was large, with separate bedrooms for each of the children, and when a smaller studio apartment adjacent to their own had become available, they bought it, too, breaking through the wall so that Robert could have a study at home.

He must have liked working at home. He was known as a fond husband and loving father. Some of Irene's friends told me that while they always gossiped about whose marriage was in what creaking condition, there was never any gossip about Irene and Robert, who had been married for ten years. And one of the family's baby-sitters, an eighteen-year-old who often worked for them, said, "They were extremely close. They were always holding hands." Robert's hobby was amateur photography, and one of his favorite subjects was his family. His study walls were lined with pictures of the two smiling children and of Irene, a pretty woman who wore her curly hair to her shoulders and, eschewing makeup, had a natural, modest air.

She was utterly devoted to Joshua and Judy. She'd attended college, received an M.A. in education from New York University, and taught school for a while before she had the children. But once she became a mother, she gave up the notion of working outside her home. Instead, she channeled her skills at guiding and caring for the young into ministering to her own progeny.

It was an unusual choice in the early 1970s, when most women were clamoring to work. But certainly it was one with a long history of distinguished practitioners, and Irene, according to her friends, excelled at it. She spent virtually all her time with her children and was active in their schools. Both children attended private schools—different ones—and Irene participated regularly in the parents' groups at both. She was also enormously protective of her children. One friend said that what struck her most about Irene was that whenever she saw her out walking with her son and daughter, she was holding their hands tightly clasped in hers. Another said that at a swimming pool to which she and Irene belonged, Irene, unlike the other mothers, would never let her children swim with the lifeguard's supervision alone but would herself stand interminably and patiently in the shallow end of the pool until they had finished disporting themselves.

Among the other examples her friends gave to illustrate her painstaking mothering was the fact that she never failed to escort her children to and from school, never sloughed the task off onto maids and babysitters, though she could well have afforded to do so. They said further that unlike so many mothers of young children, she wasn't given to procrastination. She'd mail the children's tuition deposits to their schools well before the start of each semester and make appointments for their pediatric checkups in sufficient time for the required medical forms to reach their schools before, not on, the first day of classes.

Indeed, anticipating her son's and daughter's needs was second nature to Irene. Once, when she was to be away from home for a while, she warned her children's teachers weeks before her departure so that they could plan for the possibility that the children might miss her and thus act out or cut up or just behave differently.

But if she was protective of her own children, she was also greatly protective and fond of children in general. Whenever her friends had scheduling problems and couldn't pick up their children at school or couldn't be at home with them in the afternoons, it was always Irene to whom they would turn for help. She invariably came to their rescue, absorbing their kids into her own household for play and snacks. In fact, the very day before she took her own and her children's lives, she had arranged to care, the next day, for a child whose mother was preoccupied with a sick baby.

No wonder that to the outside world Irene Schwartz looked like Supermom.

It would have pleased her to be remembered this way. Apparently, she had set out to be a perfect mother, an available, responsive, uncomplaining maternal figure. No doubt it was because she knew what it was like to be deprived of such a bulwark. When she was a child, her own mother had often been away from home. She had suffered some kind of mental breakdown and was frequently hospitalized in psychiatric institutions.

After her mother died—it was in 1977—Irene grew extremely despondent. She saw a psychiatrist but became increasingly depressed. Ultimately, in the spring of 1980, she herself was hospitalized and given shock therapy—a tratment used frequently in cases where psychiatrists have established that a patient has suicidal yearnings. Most of her friends didn't know about her depression and its treatment.

It is here that the story of Irene Schwartz begins to take its tragic turn. After her hospitalization and as a result of the treatment, she began to improve. The summer before she died, she was no longer brooding, and on occasion she even worked as a volunteer at her children's day camp. To her doctors, she seemed well enough to be maintained on antidepressive medications as an outpatient; to her husband, well enough for him to leave her for a short while to go to Europe to attend an economics conference. But it is one of the commonplaces of psychiatry, and one of the aspects of the discipline that most demoralizes its practitioners, that it is often only when severely depressed, potentially suicidal patients are on the upswing, only when they show signs of being less melancholy and once again taking an interest in the world around them, that they can organize themselves sufficiently to carry out an exit from the earth. All psychiatrists dread this ironic fact and fear the responsibility of caring for the severely depressed.

This was the case with Irene Schwartz. Her father said to me, "No one knew what she was planning. Not just the outsiders. Even we, her family. I spent the Saturday before her death with her and the children. She was laughing. The children were laughing. Yes, she was in treatment. But no one suspected anything like this at the time."

In her final hours, Irene Schwartz must have missed her mother and longed to be reunited with her, for she left a note saying that she wanted to be with her mother. She also wrote that she was afraid that unless she joined her mother now, she too might have to spend her days in hospitals. And then she picked up the shotgun.

That Irene Schwartz should have wanted to kill herself, given her history of severe depression, seems comprehensible. Suicide among depressed people is twenty-five times greater than among the population at large. But the children? What makes a loving mother, however depressed, murder her offspring?

I asked several authorities on female depression to explain this phenomenon. "There are several components," Dr. Helen Kaplan, clinical professor of psychiatry at Cornell Medical Center, told me. "One of them is rage. When you talk about an infanticide, as opposed to a suicide, it isn't really enough to talk merely about depression. Think of Medea. There's no better way to do your husband in than to kill not just yourself but your children. It's better than suicide, because if *you* die, your husband will eventually forget about you. No matter how much he loved you, he'll eventually marry again, and he won't even have to pay alimony. But if you obliterate the children, you can be sure he'll remember you to the end of his days."

Dr. Alexandra Symonds, a psychiatrist who has worked at New York's Bellevue Hospital with women who killed their children and then tried to kill themselves but survived, concurred with Dr. Kaplan but stressed that her patients had usually not been aware of the rage component. "It wasn't just that they denied it," she said. "They actually *believed* they were saving their children from, say, the devil, or that they had to kill them because there was no one around who would look after them once they themselves were gone. They were delusional."

Maggie Scarf, author of *Unfinished Business: Pressure Points in the Lives of Women*, suggested to me that in the case of Irene Schwartz "there may have been a blurring of the boundaries between herself and her children." Some psychic blurring goes on during pregnancy, when a child is in its mother's womb, and during early infancy. At those times it's normal, perhaps even essential, for the well-being of the child. "But later on," she said, "a woman *has* to recognize that there are boundaries, has to know that when her child feels bad it doesn't mean she has to feel bad, or that when she feels bad, her child needn't. If a mother can't separate herself from her children, it's pathological."

Clearly Irene Schwartz, who had devoted her life to her children, had blurred the boundaries between herself and them and had come to believe that there was no one to look after them once she died. That this was a delusion that didn't even approach reality is what makes her story so painful, for consider this: at her funeral services, held jointly with those for the children, the chapel was thronged with relatives and friends. Many of them, had Irene only been well enough to communicate her fears, might willingly have volunteered to raise and coddle Judy and Joshua. There was Irene's father, her in-laws, and a host of aunts, uncles, and cousins. And, of course, her husband.

He rose before the assembled mourners and spoke out in a heartrending but steady voice. "My daughter, Judy, was precious in every way," he began. Then, with a father's awareness of a child's most intimate affections and habits, he told the group that Judy had had a favorite song, one she listened to on her phonograph each night before she went to sleep. The song was "Tomorrow," from *Annie*, with its exuberant melody and buoyant lyrics. He'd found the record there on her child-size phonograph the morning he'd been summoned precipitately home from Europe. "I love ya, tomorrow . . . Just thinking about tomorrow clears away the cobwebs and sorrow till there's none."

As for his son, "Josh was a dynamo," Robert Schwartz said. "For the rest of my life, Josh, I'll be a better man because of you, little buddy."

The desolation in the stunned man's voice was almost unendurable. Those mourners who had not cried earlier began weeping inconsolably until at last a rabbi, the very one who had married Irene and Robert, tried to stem the sobbing by seeking to explain how so loving a mother could have performed so desperate an act. "It was not Irene who did what was done," said the rabbi. "It was the illness which overwhelmed her and her life. . . . Who can comprehend the power of the disease?"

I left the funeral that afternoon thinking obsessively about my teenage daughter and how, when she'd been little and mischievous, I'd frequently snapped, "Do that again and I'll kill you!" How often had it happened? How often, when she and her friends had played their favorite games—Tent, which involved burying masses of clothes and toys and even food and drink under a canopy created by a bedspread on the floor; Swimming Pool, which involved filling pots and pans with water and spreading the vessels out on the carpet for Barbie dolls to swim in and little girls to knock over—how often in those days had I said to my husband when he came home, "I came within an inch of killing the kids this afternoon."

But that inch was really a mile. There is an enormous divide that separates the normal mother from the infanticide. It can be an alarming, lonely space, a daunting desert that makes a mother say of her children, "I just can't understand them. They're nothing like me." But it is what keeps our children safe.

THE TRANSSEXUAL, THE BARTENDER, AND THE SUBURBAN PRINCESS

Rockland County, New York

1981

The Hudson River washes up a hundred or so bodies a year. It is New York's Ganges, the watery resting place of numerous dead, many the victims of stabbings and shootings. The identities of these victims and of their assailants frequently remain unknown. But when, on October 28, 1981, a woman's body, dressed in a lavender spaghetti-strap camisole and lavender pants, wrapped in a yellowish water-sodden blanket, and riddled with four bullet holes in the skull, was fished from the river at West Twenty-eighth Street, the body was quickly identified, largely because there was something most unusual about it.

Examining the lavender-garbed corpse, doctors at the city's medical examiner's office discovered that it belonged to no ordinary female. The vagina was abnormally large, there were no ovaries or uterus, and there was a telltale bit of prostate gland. They informed Manhattan detectives of these anomalies, and the detectives, who had already begun checking on missing persons in and around New York, began to suspect that the body belonged to a twenty-four-year-old named Diane Delia, who had disappeared from her home in Yonkers. Diane, they had learned, had been a woman for only a short while. Indeed, until a year before she had been John Delia, a man.

So began one of the most bizarre criminal cases of our era. It resulted, after a three-month investigation, in the indictment of two people: a well-to-do, twenty-six-year-old doctor's daughter named Robyn Arnold, who had purportedly been engaged to marry Delia when he was still a man, and a twenty-two-year-old, down-at-the-heels bartender named Robert Ferrara, who had actually married Delia once he became a woman. It led to a tension-filled murder trial and a dramatic verdict. But what proved most intriguing of all about this odd case was the door it opened on a style of life in a corner of suburbia few people knew existed.

Philip Roth once observed that the American writer in the mid-twentieth century has his hands full trying to comprehend and then make believable much of American reality. "The actuality," he wrote, "is continually outdoing our talents, and the culture tosses up figures almost daily that are the envy of any novelist." I thought of Roth's words constantly as I began my immersion in the case of John/Diane Delia and his/her best beloveds.

I started my research by visiting a disco called Zipperz, in New Rochelle, New York, on a Saturday night about a year after Delia's body had been hauled from the river. I'd heard that John/Diane Delia had been well known at Zipperz, where, long before he altered his body to make it female, he used to do female impersonations. His impersonation of Diana Ross was famous in his crowd, and indeed, after the disco learned he had been murdered, it sponsored a kind of memorial service for him—a John/Diane

Delia night during which a pride of female impersonators mimicked Delia mimicking Ross.

Zipperz was a gay disco, catering to both sexes,
and the clientele for the most part was young, unsophisticated, and employed at unskilled, low-paying
jobs. The night I was there, I met an abundance of
sales clerks, waiters, and waitresses, hair stylists and
manicurists. "Most of the people here are just coming
out," one muscular hair stylist explained. "Some of
them are still in high school, and some of them are
just starting their careers, just beginning to look for
jobs."

The place was jammed that Saturday, the dance
floor teeming, the lines at the bar three deep. Behind
the barroom itself was another area, a large, dark
room with low-slung couches set into little cubicles.
On the couches, couples or threesomes were
sprawled in complicated embraces. "It's not polite to
look," the hair stylist chided as he showed me
through the room.

I'd never been in a place like Zipperz before, and at
first I felt uneasy, sure that none of its patrons would
want to talk to me, an outsider. But, to my surprise, I
found that as soon as I explained that I was there
because I wanted to write about the Delia case, I was
deluged with communicants. Delia had apparently
been everyone's favorite transsexual—although this,
said a lesbian who claimed to have been a good friend
of the deceased, "is a distinction not unlike being
everyone's favorite concentration camp guard. Transsexuals as a bunch are not a very nice bunch."

It was this woman who told me that Delia had
been an extraordinarily talented impersonator. She'd
seen him do Diana Ross not just here, at Zipperz, but

in a Manhattan club called the Ice Palace. "He was beautiful," she said. "Tall, olive-skinned, with long dark hair streaked with red highlights. And then he'd put on this Diana Ross wig, a really expensive wig, and he would just *become* Diana Ross. It was magical. I've seen lots of female impersonators, but he was far and away the best."

Another woman disagreed about Delia's abilities, pointing out that he never actually sang during his shows but lip-synched to a recording. "He was only so-so," she muttered. "Nothing special."

"She's just jealous," said a man in a curly blond wig. "Ask them over at the Playroom about Diane Delia. Or at the Talk of the Town. Or even down in the city, at Studio Fifty-four. Diane Delia was a *star!*"

I did ask around about Delia that night, visiting a number of the suburban gay bars and discos where he/she had been a regular. I was denied entry to the Talk of the Town on the edge of Scarsdale, a fancy establishment whose parking lot was overflowing with Mercedes-Benzes and BMWs. "No women," the man at the door informed me. "I don't care what you've heard about us. We just don't let women in, no matter who they once were." But I spent some time at the Playroom in Yonkers, a dingy bar on a side street where I noticed that several of the female customers were wearing what was apparently the latest in S-M jewelry, lightweight metal chains looped together like strands of pearls. And it was that night that I first realized how provincial I, a New Yorker, was. All the clubs I toured were doing a land office business, yet I had assumed that the kinds of night spots in which transsexuals hung out were a big-city phenomenon, that in the suburbs life was still just a matter of tricycles and skating ponds, commuter schedules and gray flannel suits.

Delia had been born in Riverdale, New York, the second son of Joan and Bruno Delia, a builder. He had been an Rh-negative baby, and within hours of his birth he had had to be transfused—an event that he embued with great significance. Years later he told his girlfriend Robyn Arnold that his blood type may have determined his entire future, for his mother, perhaps because of the slim thread upon which his existence had momentarily hung, forever after pampered him, made him her darling. Certainly, he never had quite the same childhood as his older brother, a macho youth who used to hang around Bruno Delia's construction sites. Joan Delia kept John at home with her. There, according to Robyn, she played with him when he was a preschooler as if he were a little girl, dressing him in her clothes, styling his hair, dabbing makeup on his cheeks. Later, she taught him to clean the house, shop for groceries, cook.

Was his subsequent interest in cross dressing and, ultimately, in switching his sex the result of these early environmental experiences? Or was there something about him, some ineffable and subtle difference from other boys, that inspired his mother to treat him more like a female than a male? The answer is unknowable. Nor do psychiatrists, psychologists, an medical researchers agree about whether sexual confusion emanates from nurture or nature. All that is certain in this case is that by the time John Delia entered high school, he felt himself emphatically different from other adolescent males. In his closet, he had a collection of women's frivolous dresses.

* * *

He attended Manhattan's High School of Art & Design, showing talent in art and music. But eventually music took over. "Our whole family is very musical," Joan Delia explained. "My oldest son plays five instruments. I myself used to sing light opera. But Diane"—she called her youngest Diane, whereas his father consistently referred to him as John—"was the best of the lot of us. She had a beautiful voice. Teeth like Liberace! Eyes like black olives! A personality, a charisma, that stole the show."

It wasn't just John's mother who thought his personality charismatic. Several people who knew him described him as unique and compelling, noting in particular that he had a vibrant sense of humor. It was the kind of humor that has become almost a clichéd style among drag queens, mocking and derisive. When a black man, noticing him walking the streets dressed as Diana Ross, said to him, "You're a disgrace to the black race," John tittered, "You're a disgrace to the *human* race." When some men in a diner noticed him sitting there dressed in drag and began commenting aloud on whether or not he was a female, he opened his shirt and, flashing a hormone-induced breast, giggled, "This ain't real?" His humor was insistent, inescapable, and his manner outgoing and forceful. "He just had this *way* about him," was how Robyn Arnold put it. "He was the kind of person who could get you to do anything he wanted, even if you didn't want to do it. If you were tired after work and wanted to stay at home and he wanted to go out and have a good time, somehow before you knew it you'd be getting dressed and ready for an evening out."

John's personality had a negative side, however.

Like many transsexuals, he seems to have had the psychiatric disorder once known as hysteria and today called histrionic-personality disorder, a disturbance marked by highly emotional, demanding, and impulsive behavior. In an article in the *American Journal of Psychiatry*, the psychiatrist Paul Chodoff vividly described the histrionic personality as "attention-seeking and sexually seductive," noting, however, that hysterical seductiveness "has a superficial quality and is not, in fact, intensely erotic." Further, he explained, hysterics have a poor grasp on reality. Not only do they act as if they were always onstage, but "they may become so carried away by their performances that they have difficulty in distinguishing fantasy from reality." In addition, they have "strong and often unbridled dependency needs" that manifest themselves in clinging and demanding relationships with other people.

Chodoff might have been describing John Delia. He was always onstage, always calling attention to himself. Performing in drag before his sex change operation, he'd wear nothing beneath his dresses and, sitting, would cross and uncross his legs to display his genitals. After the operation, he would invite anyone who cared to look to examine his bandages and, once they were removed, his new biology.

He was wildly possessive. Robyn Arnold told me, "If we were in a bar and some other guys started talking to me, he'd storm through three rooms to pull me away from them."

Above all, he was fond of scenes. He'd fly into rages. He'd get into street brawls. And he'd threaten suicide. "Delia was always making these theatrics all the time," said Dominick Giorgio, a male nurse who knew Delia as both John and Diane and was a key witness at the murder trial. "She was always threatening to slash her wrists. Or to kill herself some other way. One time she jumped off a third-story terrace. Naturally, she didn't get hurt. You just knew she'd planned it out, because she managed to land right in the middle of the bushes under the terrace."

John's hysterical nature became most apparent, however, in his efforts to settle on a sexual identity, a matter that for most of us is a given. He hurtled between indentities the way a trapeze artist flies between bars, hoping that in grasping hold, the void would be transcended. But somehow John's reach kept exceeding his grasp.

By the time he was twenty-one, he was an avowed homosexual. He'd had affairs with a number of men, among them Robert Ferrara, a bartender he'd met at the Playroom. But it was around that time that he began to feel, as transsexuals almost always say they feel, that he was not just a man who enjoyed having sex with other men but that—somewhere deep inside—he was a woman. He began seeing a psychiatrist, to whom he disclosed his intention of becoming a woman anatomically by having a sex change operation. He also started taking the hormone shots that gave him breasts. And he decided to get some plastic surgery so that he would appear more delicate. He'd had a couple of operations already, one to exaggerate his cheekbones, another to reduce his Adam's apple. Now he determined to get himself a pretty nose.

He seemed set on his course to become female until, when he was twenty-two, he met Robyn Arnold, after which, suddenly, his sexual focus changed. He began courting Robyn, who was the prototype of a suburban princess. The daughter of an ear, nose, and throat surgeon, she had been given sixteen years of ballet lessons, a Cadillac with the license plate ROBYN-1, and an $80,000 inheritance from her grandfather, a pediatrician. She found Delia intriguing. "I'd never met anyone quite like him," she said later.

John stopped taking hormone shots and began lifting weights, hoping it would discourage his blossoming breasts. And the two became lovers.

Within weeks after they met, John and Robyn were an established couple. Bruno, John's father, and Patricia, his stepmother, were amazed but delighted. On Valentine's Day 1980, they invited the young couple to have dinner with them, and they beamed when they heard that John had presented Robyn with a pair of sapphire earrings.

By early spring, the families of the young lovers were getting acquainted. Robyn's parents invited Bruno and Patricia Delia to join the big gathering of Arnold cousins, aunts, and uncles at their Passover celebration. The mingling went well and when, at the dinner, Bruno said his construction company was becoming prosperous and would soon be putting up an elegant condominium, Robyn's parents discussed investing some of their daughter's money in the project.

Later that spring, Robyn went to California with John. Although he was by this time something of a celebrity at the Westchester nightclubs and had even begun to be invited to perform at some major league Manhattan discos, he had made up his mind that he wanted something bigger and better for himself than the life of an entertainer. He wanted to be a famous model or, better yet, a movie star.

On the West Coast, he tried to land a movie role, but he had no luck. Indeed, the only job he could find was as a market researcher. Robyn may have felt disillusioned with him, for she returned to New York. Yet their affair wasn't over, for John came home soon afterward, saw Robyn, and announced to his parents and everyone else who would listen that he and Robyn were going to get married.

The Arnolds took the news badly. It was one thing to socialize with the Delias, altogether another to envision their daughter marrying John. They called Bruno Delia and demanded that he discourage the match. But to Bruno it looked as if his mixed-up son had finally straightened out. He didn't try to talk him out of marrying Robyn; instead, he and his wife made plans to take John and his sweetheart to their country club.

Unknown to the Delias, however, their erratic son had by then once again begun changing his mind about sexuality. His urge to become a woman had returned. He discussed the problem with Robyn, and she agreed that if he wanted a sex change operation he ought to have it. At last, in November 1980, at the age of twenty-three, John flew to Trinidad, Colorado, where he underwent an operation called a penile inversion.

Dr. Stanley Biber performed the intricate surgery. He removed John's penis and testicles and, creating a cavity precisely where a woman would have a vagina, used John's penile skin to line it and his glans penis to give it a cervix. He made a set of inner and outer vaginal lips out of John's scrotal skin and a clitoris out of his penile erectile tissue.

The operation cost John about $5,000. It took two and a half hours.

She—for now it is necessary to change the personal pronoun—telephoned Robyn after the surgery, complaining about being in pain and feeling disoriented. And she told her drag queen friends that she simply couldn't get used to the unfortunate way in which women urinated. But taking the name Diane, after her favorite subject of impersonation, she soon cheerfully began trying to exist as a woman.

She had some luck in this. She went off to Canada, and got a job as hostess in a Montreal nightclub. Prospering, she frequently came back to New York to see her friends, and when she did, they noticed that she often arrived with a great deal of cocaine. Then, not long after the operation, she won her first—and only—modeling assignment, a catalogue shot for Avon Products. In a photograph that was eventually to become famous—after her murder, it was splashed across tabloids throughout the United States—Diane posed awkwardly in a nylon bathrobe. "Wrap yourself in luxury," read the copy. "Totally irresistible..." (The ad caused Avon vast embarrassment, but it brought Diane, albeit after her death, the kind of recognition she had longed for.)

Her career was under way. But if the operation had made it possible for her start making a living as a female, it had not in any way made it easier for her to feel more comfortable about herself or put an end to her attention-seeking and seductive behavior. Indeed, now more than ever she seemed to need the sexual validation craved by the histrionic personality, a validation that is most often sought in the indiscriminate seduction of others. Abandoning Canada, Diane came back to live in New York and began testing her new-found femininity by picking up strangers. One night, she flirted with an executive she'd met at a midtown bar; the conversation went well, and after a while he took her back to his room at the fashionable Helmsley Palace Hotel and they made love. Afterward, while the executive was in the shower, Diane quietly dialed Robyn and, whispering, boasted to her about the exploit.

But her tests of her sexuality weren't always so successful. On another night she picked up a man who asked her, right in the midst of their lovemaking, whether she'd ever been a man. Reluctantly, she told him yes. Abruptly, he got out of bed, got dressed, and left. Diane remained behind, weeping.

Perhaps it was as a result of such rejections that Diane first began considering getting married. Perhaps marriage seemed like a haven to her. Or perhaps she merely longed to be wedded just for the attention and notoriety the ceremony would bring her. Regardless, in the summer of 1981 she persuaded her old boyfriend Robert Ferrara that he ought to become her husband, and in August, the two drove out to Robert's hometown, Berwick, Pennsylvania, population 12,350, and applied for a marriage license.

The county clerk thought them a beautiful couple —the prospective groom a "handsome Berwick boy," the blush-painted bride "stacked" and wearing "one of these look-see dresses." He gave them their application, then directed them to get their blood tests and return after the four days the law required.

On Sunday night, they came back to Berwick and told Robert's parents they intended to wed. The Ferraras tried to talk them out of it. They knew Diane's sexual background. "For hours, we sat around the kitchen table and talked and talked," Robert's mother told me. "There was no arguing. No yelling. Just a lengthy exchange of deep talk." But Diane and Robert wouldn't change their minds, so at last the Ferraras felt they had no choice but to accept the arrangement.

Still, there was some trouble. When Diane and Robert went to pick up their marriage license the next day, the county clerk at first refused to give it to them. A neighbor of the Ferraras, having learned of the proposed marriage, had told him, "That's a boy marrying a boy." The clerk had alerted the sheriff and the deputy sheriff, who were standing by. But Delia's operation had entitled her to become a woman legally as well as structurally. She had brought proof of the operation in the form of an affidavit signed by Dr. Biber; she even had a new birth certificate, with John's date of birth but her female name of Diane. The clerk succumbed to the evidence and handed the couple their license.

After that, it was roses all the way. The couple proceeded to the town's justice of the peace. Robert's parents and a brother went along. And Robert and Diane swiftly became man and wife.

The groom seemed to be like the "usual groom," the justice of the peace later commented, and there was nothing especially unusual about the bride, either. In fact, the only thing that struck him as out of the ordinary was that the groom's father had seemed "relieved." He'd paid the justice's $10 fee out of his own pocket, remarking that it was the best investment he'd ever made in his life.

The union had Robyn Arnold's blessing. She paid for the ring, a $1,400 cluster of three gold bands ornamented with seven diamonds.

For Diane, it was a storybook beginning to yet another new life. But this life ran no more smoothly than the others she had tried. Soon, she and her bridegroom were quarreling. He was turned off by her new sex. Yet she, more than ever, needed sexual approval, so just as in her single days, she went on having affairs. And just as in her single days, the affairs didn't always make her happy. One night, she tried to have intercourse with a friend from Zipperz, an auto parts salesman named Bobby Vasquez, but he kept thinking, he would eventually explain, that "she'd been a man," and he couldn't go through with it. The incident made Diane intensely anxious.

With her characteristic impulsiveness, Diane finally decided her unhappiness was somehow being caused by her marriage and that she had best move out of her home with Robert in Yonkers and once again make her life with Robyn Arnold. Thus, on October 4, 1981, Vasquez, as well as a Zipperz DJ named Tony Poveromo and a hair stylist named Laura Schultz, helped Diane move her belongings from the shabby nuptial nest she had shared with Robert to Robyn Arnold's chic Riverdale apartment.

The move set off two days of partying. First, Robyn welcomed the movers enthusiastically and then, upon being invited to join the group, decided to change her clothes and go out with them. She slipped out of her jeans and, according to Vasquez, who was just carrying in a heavy armload of Diane's wigs and gowns, pointed at her private parts and said invitingly, "Mine are real. Not like Delia's." Then they all went off to a diner for coffee, where they chattered and tittered and came on to one another. Robyn squeezed one of Vasquez's thighs under the table while Diane squeezed the other, and everyone got on famously.

The partying continued out in the parking lot of the diner, but now Diane complicated the evening by flirting with Laura, the hair stylist, hugging and kissing her right in the parking lot. Diane had turned lesbian, her friends remarked.

No one seemed to mind. Diane's outrageousness was amusing, irreverent. It made the evening click, keep clicking. They were a group on the go, a quintet that didn't want the magic to stop. That night, everyone slept at Robyn's.

The group's pleasure in each other's company continued, turned even more heady. The next day the party went on, moving to Tony's. Robyn didn't join in, but everyone else showed up, and they stayed awake late and fell asleep locked in one another's arms. Diane had forgotten all about her miserable marriage. But the next night she was ready to face up to her problems, and when her husband, Robert, said he wanted to get together with her to talk about whether they could iron out their difficulties, she agreed to meet him.

Robert, driving Robyn's car, came to Tony's to fetch Diane, who dressed fetchingly for the rendezvous in a lavender spaghetti-strap camisole, lavender pants, and purple suede heels. It was the last time anyone in the group would see her. She never returned from her talk with Robert, and three months later Robert was arrested and indicted for killing her. Oddly, so too was Robyn Arnold. They'd acted together to get rid of Diane, read the indictment.

I attended the pretrial hearings in Manhattan Supreme Court and, later, the trial itself, and from the beginning I kept struggling to try to understand what had drawn Robert and Robyn to the mercurial John/ Diane Delia. I also kept struggling to understand what—aside from their both finding, for a time, a lover and soulmate in Delia—they could possibly have in common. It was clear that there was *something*. After Delia disappeared, the two lived together, sharing Robyn's apartment. And in court, at least during the pretrial sessions, they behaved like friends, smiling at and chatting with one another. Yet they seemed remarkably different.

Robyn was clearly a royal being, her auburn hair lustrous, her fingernails impeccably manicured, her body tanned and athletic, her stylish tops and flowing skirts different every day. Unlike Robert, she was out on $25,000 bail, and whenever she came to court she was engulfed by family: her father, the surgeon; her mother, an administrator in the father's East Side office; a clutch of concerned cousins and aunts; even, after a while, a new financé, a Manhattan dentist. She would laugh and giggle with these people or with her expensive lawyer, Michael Rosen of Saxe, Bacon & Bolan, the firm headed by Roy Cohn, as if being in court was just another stop in her easy round of pleasant, self-pampering rituals. She was either stalwartly secure in her innocence or completely without a sense of appropriate behavior. It was hard to imagine her in love with Delia.

Robert was another type altogether—depressed, anxious, clearly less prosperous, for he was always in the same suit. And he had no hangers-on in the courtroom, not even any family. His mother told me that he'd asked his parents not to attend the trial, saying it would be too painful and shocking. Still, she'd wanted to come anyway and would have, she said, except that just before the trial began, she finally—after eight months of looking—found a job in Berwick. She added, "Besides, New York is a four-and-a-half-hour drive each way, and if I didn't drive each day, where could I have afforded to stay over?"

For a moment, I was touched. Then I remembered that Robert's lawyer had said that after the marriage to Delia, the family had disowned him, decided they wanted nothing further to do with him.

As I began to learn about Robert and Robyn, I saw that it was relatively easy to understand Delia's appeal for the bartender.

Robert was brought up in Rockland County, New York, but before he completed his senior year of high school, his family moved to Berwick. "We had to move because of economic reasons," his mother explained. Robert finished high school in Berwick, but he was exceedingly unhappy in the tiny town. The Ferrara home, a split-level ranch house, was in a rural area on three acres of land that bordered a big field, where wealthier neighbors kept horses. Behind it stretched woods and hills and, beyond them, more woods and hills. Robert made up his mind to get out of Pennsylvania.

He joined the navy but realized that it wasn't for him and went AWOL. Disappearing from his base in San Diego, he returned to the New York suburbs and tried to elude discovery. He lived with friends, worked as a waiter, then started tending bar. He was fixing drinks at the Playroom in 1978 when he met John Delia and first became his lover.

He rarely had any money. Robyn Arnold said she lived with Robert after Delia disappeared only because he couldn't pay his rent in Yonkers; she took him in because she had taken pity on him. And according to his friend, the nurse Dominick Giorgio, his lack of money was a particular stress for he had a drug habit, relying heavily (when he could afford them) on cocaine and Quaaludes. "Delia knew this," Giorgio told me, "and one time, after a trip to Canada, she gave Ferrara a thousand dollars' worth of uncut cocaine. She had all these little bottles and gave him the bottles, too, so he could sell some of the cocaine for a hundred dollars a bottle. She said it was a present for him, so he could buy himself a motorcycle."

Delia looked after Robert, but she also fought with him. And he fought back. One night, when she wanted to go out and he wanted her to stay home, he smacked her around and threw the dishes at her. Another time, when she caught him in a car with someone else and demanded he get out, he came out swinging and knocked her to the ground, slamming her head against the sidewalk. One night at the Come Back, in Piermont, after Delia got so angry with Robert that she stabbed him in the elbow with a knife, he smashed her in the leg with a hammer. In this battle the police were called in, and Delia was jailed until her mother bailed her out, while Robert—his desertion from the navy surfacing—was sent back to California and briefly placed in the brig. When he got out, he returned to Delia and the fast New York life.

Robert and Delia had a lot in common besides explosive tempers. Like Delia, Robert had hopes of becoming a model, a male model. He jogged and lifted weights and eventually put together a portfolio of flattering photographs. Like Delia, he was fond of clothes, although where Delia favored skirts and shirts trimmed with maribou feathers, he liked designer jeans and Lacoste polo shirts. And, like Delia, he had been unsettled about his sexuality. After their first affair, he lived for a time with a young woman from Berwick—although he continued to see Delia.

Finally, Robert and Delia were alike in one other, important way. Each one was prone to hysterical suicide attempts. One day, a few months after Diane disappeared, Robert nearly succeeded in doing away with himself. Downing a fat handful of Quaaludes, he took a cab to the Red Carpet Inn in Paramus, New Jersey, and there tried to die by smashing a glass ashtray and cutting his wrists with the shards.

Robyn Arnold's fascination with Delia was more difficult to untangle, for on the surface, at least, they seemed nothing alike. Robyn had been born in Manhattan but raised from the time she was four in a big, comfortable house in the Westchester suburb of Mount Vernon. Several young women who knew her during her grammar school years there told me she had not been popular. They said she used to walk off with their toys. The mother of one of these girls recalled a day when her daughter and some other children decided they no longer wanted to play with Robyn. They relented only after Mrs. Arnold approached this woman and asked her to intercede on behalf of the outcast.

But on the whole Robyn seemed to have had a pleasant, indulgent girlhood. Besides her ballet lessons, she studied music, attended cousins-club meetings and country clubs with her parents, went to mother-and-daughter luncheons at a synagogue in Mount Vernon, learned to ski and play tennis, and became an inveterate shopper. Her last two high school years were spent at a private school in Tarrytown. Still, she must have been a troubled adolescent. At some point in her high school days, she was involved in a petty theft that brought her to the attention of the police, but since she was a juvenile, her records were sealed.

When it came time to choose a profession, Robyn decided on nursing. Her whole family was involved in medicine. Not only was her father a doctor, but her grandfather had been one too. Her favorite cousin was a nurse, and her only sibling, a brother, was planning to go to medical school. Robyn enrolled at Lehman College, in the Bronx, determined to become a nurse.

This much about her is clear. Other areas of her life are more murky. For example, the women who went to school with her in Mount Vernon told me she had changed her name to Robyn from the less glamorous Roberta. Indeed, one of her relatives, whom I interviewed during the trial, kept referring to her as Roberta. But Robyn insisted that she hadn't changed her name and that she was never known as Roberta. Moreover, she originally told me that before going to Lehman College, she got a B.S. degree from Syracuse University. Syracuse reported that no student named Robyn *or* Roberta Arnold had ever earned a degree there. (When asked about this discrepancy, Robyn insisted that she had attended Syracuse, but just for two years. Syracuse then informed me that a Roberta Arnold had attended for a single semester before dropping out.) Robyn also said she was a licensed nurse, but the New York State Division of Professional Licensing said, in a phone interview, that their records did not disclose a registered or practical nurse named either Robyn or Roberta Arnold.

After Lehman College, Robyn landed a nursing job at Montefiore Hospital, in the Bronx. She is vague about what happened next. For some reason, she and Montefiore parted company, and she took a job with a plastic surgeon. It was in his office, according to her, that she met Delia. But there are two scenarios for that meeting. Delia's friends told police, after Delia was murdered, that Robyn used to frequent the Playroom and that she and Delia met there. No matter. By the end of 1979, they were dating.

Then came the courtship. There are also two versions of that. The Delias, mother Joan, stepmother Patricia, and father Bruno, all claimed that Robyn and John were engaged and that they even went for a premarital blood test. Robyn told me that wasn't true and said that although she and John were lovers, they hadn't made wedding plans. "I'd *never* have married Delia," she said. "He was too confused a person." She also said that John had told his parents a lot of stories about her that weren't true, among them that he'd made her pregnant and that she'd gotten an abortion, during which it was discovered that she had been carrying twins. None of this was correct, Robyn insisted. John had made up the story to make himself appear, once he was dating a woman, highly macho.

Robyn, of course, did not marry John. But they remained friends, and eventually she managed his career, booking his dates, buying his costumes, even opening a joint checking account with him. And she became the friend of his friends. Why? What was a girl of her background doing in a world like that? Her favorite cousin, Connie, told me, "Robyn was going through a period of reduced ego. Delia and his friends made her feel good." A close friend from nursing school, Barbara Barlow, had a somewhat different explanation. "Robyn was always looking for the ultimate thrill," she said. "She did everything to try to get it."

After Delia disappeared, Robyn stayed close to her onetime lover's friends, inviting them to a Christmas party, lending them Delia's clothes, and living with Robert. She even traveled with Robert to Fort Lauderdale, Florida, and spent time there with him and a female impersonator who had become so attached to Delia that he called Delia "my sister." The affectionate impersonator claimed that Robyn was "forever taking" Black Beauties—amphetamines—and that she also took LSD one night, only to appear crying and distraught the next morning and to demand of him, "Bobby Ferrara said I told you last night that we—or I—killed Diane. Did I?" The impersonator assured her that she hadn't. (Robyn denied the incident to me; she also denied ever taking drugs.)

Meanwhile, the police were questioning Delia's friends, and their investigation began to focus more and more on Robyn and Robert. One member of the circle handed over a pair of enormous purple suede shoes that appeared to be the ones in which Delia had last teetered about. The shoes had come from Robyn's closet. Other friends began telling the police that Robert had been furious with Delia for moving out and that Robyn had been furious with Delia for moving in and then promptly flirting with Laura. The clincher came for the police, however, after Dominick Giorgio was picked up for stealing synthetic cocaine from Pascack Valley Hospital, in Westwood, New Jersey, where he worked in the emergency room. He eventually told detectives that he'd heard both Robyn and Robert admit to Delia's murder. They were arrested within a week.

When the pretrial hearings were finally over and the trial itself got under way, Robyn at last appeared to realize the gravity of her situation. She began ignoring Robert's bids for conversation, and after a while the two of them sat at the defense table like mismatched strangers in a crowded restaurant who have been dropped at the same table by a sardonic headwaiter.

* * *

The trial lasted four weeks and turned out to be a remarkable drama, featuring extraordinary witnesses, an eleventh-hour confession, and a cliffhanging, four-day jury deliberation. It was also, at times, sheer theater of the absurd. The major players were no longer Robyn and Robert but Judge Harold Rothwax, of Manhattan Supreme Court; Assistant District Attorney Steve Saracco; Robyn's defense attorney, Rosen; and Robert's defense attorney, Robert Dilts, of Ridgewood, New Jersey.

Each person had reasons of his own to consider the case exceptionally challenging. For Rothwax, the challenge was that the two defendants were being tried together. This is done in New York when evidence *links* two defendants. In this case, one of the chief pieces of evidence would be the testimony of nurse Giorgio, who claimed to have heard each defendant separately confess that they'd murdered Delia and that they'd done it together. Because of this link, Rothwax felt legally bound to refuse defense requests for separate trials.

But the joint-trial law has a serious drawback. It requires a jury to understand that not all evidence presented during a trial is admissible against *both* defendants. Some evidence can be held against only one. For example, if one defendant in a joint trial confesses to the crime, that confession can be held against only him, no matter what it says about the role of his codefendant. Thus, the joint-trial law goes, in effect, against a natural inclination. It demands that at one moment a jury give certain evidence serious weight and that at another the jury screen that evidence from its consciousness.

Given what he knew of human mind and memory,

Rothwax had long had doubts about the wisdom of the joint-trial law. Now he was being asked to try a case under it. In the end, he came to view the trial's outcome as a validation of the law and a vivid demonstration of a jury's ability to deliberate according to instructions. But early on he worried about whether the jury would be able to absorb the complex directions he was continually issuing.

For the Assistant D.A., Saracco, trying his thirty-eighth felony case, the murder victim herself was the challenge. During jury selection, numerous prospective jurors had snickered at the tidbits of Delia's lifestyle that were described. Saracco had begun to fear that most jurors would be incapable of feeling sufficient empathy for Deila to treat the murder with the gravity it deserved. As a result, he decided not to challenge jurors who were young or employed in the arts. "Our side usually goes for the kind of guy who hangs out in Rosie O'Grady's bar or has a big, traditional family with a lot of kids," he later explained to me. "But how could we sell *them* Delia?"

The jury that was finally selected consisted mostly of youthful, white, highly educated men and women, including three actors. But would such a jury—the kind generally considered favorable to the defense—be capable of finding the defendants guilty? Saracco kept worrying.

Robyn Arnold's counsel, Rosen, was worried because he was not planning to mount a case—in the sense of putting forward an array of witnesses or calling his client to the stand. He was hoping to win almost strictly on the basis of arduous cross-examination. But he knew how risky this approach would be: many legal observers think juries never fully accept the notion of a defendant's presumed innocence when the defendant doesn't take the stand.

The person most challenged, however, was Robert's counsel, Robert Dilts. Mild-mannered and strait-laced, Dilts, whose services were being paid for by a friend of Ferrara's from the gay community in New Jersey, often spoke of his bewilderment with the life-style the case was exposing. "Here I am, a normal guy," he mused to me outside the courtroom. "I mean, I've never had a desire to marry someone who had a fake vagina. Or even to hang out with someone who did. Or take drugs. Or go to clubs like these. I'm a normal guy. And I'm trying to understand all *this*!"

In the face of these concerns, the trial at last got under way. The prosecution contended that on the night of October 7, 1981, Robyn Arnold and Robert Ferrara drove Delia to a wooded spot in Rockland County and shot her, each firing twice. About two weeks later, according to the prosecution, Robert returned to the scene of the crime. Delia's body had not been discovered. Robert bundled Delia into a yellow blanket and dropped her into the Hudson, where she floated downstream. No murder weapon had been found, so with the exception of Giorgio, the prosecution witnesses would testify simply about Robyn and Robert's possible motives for killing Delia and about circumstantial evidence linking them to the crime.

On they came: Delia's family, her mother, step-mother, and father; Delia's pals, the habitués and managers of the bars and discos; and Delia's pro-tégés, the female impersonators (one sporting a mus-tache, another with the improbable stage name of Dottie Fuck-Fuck). The witnesses all seemed to think that both Robyn and Robert had had a motive for murder. Each of the pair, for reasons of his or her own, had become fed up with Delia.

In Robert's case, the problem had been Delia's sex change. On the verge of tears, her eyelashes fluttering, Delia's mother said that shortly before she disappeared, her daughter had telephoned and, in the long tradition of mother-bride talks, complained, "My husband isn't as active in the bedroom as he used to be." Robert, Delia's mother implied, had been disgusted by Delia's new sex and had seen no way out of the predicament of his marriage short of killing his anomalous wife.

Jealousy was suggested as Robyn's motive. Several witnesses testified that she had been obsessively in love with Delia. She had kept a kind of shrine to him, they said, with twenty or thirty photographs of him in and out of costume and all his wigs and shoes and glittery get-ups. She'd accepted his sex change, even paying for the operation, and accepted his marriage to Robert, even paying for the ring. But she'd apparently wanted to be, if not the only love of his life, at least the only woman in that life. The hair stylist Laura, with whom Delia had flirted, testified that Robyn had said wistfully to her, "If Delia can have a lesbian relationship, why can't it be with me?" Delia's stepmother, Patricia, said Robyn had told her she paid for Delia's penile inversion, and that she'd done so because "if I can't have Delia as a lover, I'd rather have him as a close girlfriend." And Delia's mother, Joan, insisted that on the night before Delia disappeared, when all the clique with the exception of Robyn had slept together at Tony Poveromo's house, Robyn had in fact gone over in the wee hours to join the group, seen Delia and Laura locked in a nude embrace, and become so enraged that she fled.

Robyn had an alibi for the hours up to about midnight on the evening Delia disappeared. She'd been getting her nails done at the home of a friend, a professional manicurist. But the prosecution claimed that she had been with Robert later that night and proved that she'd even made a telephone call for him, dialing his boss at Zipperz and saying he'd been mugged, his face was all scratched, so he wouldn't be coming to work. Other prosecution witnesses testified that Robert had pawned Delia's wedding ring, which she had presumably been wearing until she was killed; that Robyn had become furious when she'd learned that Delia's purple shoes had been taken from her; and that she'd gotten extremely shaky when a friend had pointed out that her bed was missing a familiar yellow blanket, presumably the one used to wrap Delia's dead body. (Both the shoes and the blanket became the subjects of a legal tug-of-war. *Were* the shoes the ones that Delia disappeared in? *Was* Robyn's blanket the one in which Delia's body was found?)

For the first week and a half, the evidence against both defendants was basically circumstantial. Then, as if to justify Judge Rothwax's early worries about the joint-trial law, a written confession by Robert was introduced.

It was a letter that Robert had sent to Giorgio but that Giorgio had misplaced. In fact, a friend had somehow gotten hold of it and only during jury selection thought to bring it forward.

In the letter, Robert said, "Delia had sent me and Robyn to get the gun in Pennsylvania so that she could rob some man she met at Studio Fifty-four of cocaine and cash. We would split the goods. Supposedly she would set it up when we were in

Pennsylvania. . . . Robyn, Delia and I went to Rockland to go to the Cuckoo's Nest. . . . [A friend] has supposedly stolen very expensive sound equipment from the Nest and hidden it in the woods. We arrived at the spot. Delia and I were walking toward the woods. Robyn shot her in the back of the head. I ran. [Then I came back and] I shot Delia twice to put her out of her misery."

Consternation ensued once the letter appeared. Robert didn't deny having written it, so for Dilts, his lawyer, the key would be suggesting that the letter had somehow been illegally or unethically elicited by Giorgio. For Rosen, the letter raised fears that the jury would be influenced by an assertion about his client that, while not admissible as evidence against her, might nevertheless affect their reasoning. He again demanded separate trials, but Rothwax refused.

There was no choice but to go forward, and at last Dominick Giorgio was called. He had been the recipient of the fateful letter, and if he was to be believed, he was the recipient of oral confessions to the murder by both parties on trial. Giorgio told the jury that he had heard about the murder four times. Once he had overheard Robyn say to someone on the phone, "Look, you shot her, and I shot her." Another time, she had blurted out something about the murder to Robert while Giorgio was present, then had said to Giorgio, "Now you're involved." And twice Robert had verbally confessed the act. As in the letter, he'd admitted to Giorgio that he'd shot Delia. But, said Giorgio, Robert had claimed Robyn had already shot Delia and he'd merely polished off his former beloved, as one would a wounded horse, in order to spare her further suffering.

Giorgio was the nucleus of the prosecution's case

against both defendants. But could Giorgio be believed? After Delia's disappearance, he had become Robert's lover. "He told me I was his best friend in the world," the pale, earringed male nurse said mournfully from the witness stand. Yet it was he who had told the police, after he'd been arrested for stealing drugs from the hospital, about Robert's confessing to having shot Delia. Robert had been promptly jailed, and Giorgio had received probation for his own crime. Afterward, however, they'd stayed in touch, exchanging love letters, and Giorgio had not only visited Robert in jail but once even smuggled drugs in to him. He'd been caught but had received a conditional discharge. What kind of person was he? A tormented soul or a conniving one?

Both defense attorneys insisted on the latter reading—although attributing different connivances to him. Giorgio had been no true friend to Robert, Dilts suggested, but had kept in contact with his client just in order to make him implicate *himself*—to get him, for example, to write those self-incriminating letters. Giorgio *was* Robert's creature, Rosen tried to show, and thus he'd made up the story of Robyn's involvement in the shooting, hoping that if Robert could claim Delia was already dead when he fired his shots, he might be guilty of something less than murder.

But, after all the theatrics and poses, the dramatic heart of the trial lay in the accumulation of detail about the life Delia and his friends had managed to pursue. Witness after witness reported that drugs and the kind of sexual decadence associated with cities, with Manhattan's ragged edges or Berlin's 1920s cabarets, had not only found their way to but taken root in the tranquil towns above New York. Despite their well-tended lawns and gardens, the suburbs were producing an underclass of drifting, disaffected, sensation-seeking young people. "This is the most intriguing exposé of modern suburbia anyone ever dreamed," said Rosen, the defense lawyer. "There's a legitimate subculture up there that's beyond the wildest imagination."

"You expect these things in the city," said Detective Donald Longo. "Not up there. But it turns out we're all squares in Manhattan."

Longo had hung around the gay clubs of suburbia during the investigation of the murder and had found their existence astounding. During the trial, as owners, employees, and patrons of the clubs came forward and as testimony about mood-altering drugs, orgiastic nights, and jobless days mounted, old images of suburbia began to seem like nostalgic dreams.

After three weeks of testimony, the case drew to a close. Neither defendant took the stand. In their summations, both defense attorneys focused on Giorgio. He had stolen drugs, Dilts reminded the jury, and smuggled them into Riker's Island. Given his proclivities, wasn't it possible that everything he'd said was a lie? Wasn't it even possible that the written confession itself, the one Robert had mailed Giorgio, had been elicited unscrupulously by a Giorgio who was cooperating with the police?

Attorney Rosen invented still another scenario involving Giorgio. "Imagine," he intoned, "that it's a beautiful fall day, and you and your family are taking a drive up the Palisades Parkway. Suddenly you or someone in your car has a heart attack. You wind up at Pascack Valley Hospital. You are taken to the emergency room. There, at the door, stands Dominick

Giorgio." A shiver seemed to pass through the jury, and Rosen concluded in high emotional style, "If you wouldn't trust putting your life, or that of someone in your family, into the hands of Dominick Giorgio, don't put Robyn Arnold's life in his hands, either!"

Four days later, Robyn Arnold was acquitted of the murder of Diane Delia. The jury had apparently decided not to believe Giorgio. But Robert Ferrara was convicted. The jury had apparently decided to believe Giorgio.

Several of the jurors later commented on the seeming contradiction by explaining that, basically, they had been persuaded by Rosen's argument that Giorgio had hoped to lessen Robert's guilt by dragging Robyn into the case. But at the moment of the decision, none of that mattered. Robyn's family began weeping with relief, and she herself, guilty not of murder but merely of having been a hanger-on, seemed suddenly to alter. For the first time in weeks, her control broke: her hair became disheveled, her blouse came untucked, and she acted extravagantly, nearly swooning in the arms of her lawyer. He supported her, and while he did so, Robert Ferrara was led silently away.

· Minutes later, outside the courthouse, the jury thronged Robyn. Several women jurors hugged her. She hugged them back and, her face wreathed in smiles, invited all the jurors to her upcoming wedding to the dentist. There would be a special jurors' table, she promised.

Her dentist fiancé went to get his car. Returning, he offered several of the jurors a lift uptown, and they piled in. The hubbub on the sidewalk swelled. Robyn was still surrounded. She was just starting to make excited farewells when a prison bus clanged its way up a ramp from the bowels of the courthouse and headed away down the still-crowded street. The bus was nearly empty. Inside, the only face to be seen was that of Robert Ferrara, staring.

Several days after the trial, I arranged an interview with Robyn Arnold, hoping to learn something about what it was like to escape so narrowly from being convicted of murder. But she agreed to talk only about why she'd gotten caught up with Delia and his/ her group. "I never loved him, you know," she said emphatically. Her nails were freshly manicured, her hair impeccably coiffed; she was wearing an exquisite red and purple bat-wing silk blouse. "It was just infatuation. No, not even that."

What was it, then? "It was the lifestyle," she said. "The excitement, the glamour. I found it interesting for a while. Then it grew boring." She was planning now to marry the dentist, have children, maybe even go to law school and become a defense attorney like Michael Rosen, she told me. "And I'm going to live in the suburbs. Have the life I was raised to have."

Won't that get boring, I asked, "I mean, considering the exciting life you once led?"

Robyn Arnold inspected her nails. "I've had enough excitement," she said.

THE LADY VANISHES

Nantucket Island, Massachusetts

1980

Late on a Wednesday afternoon in January 1980, an executive with Avon Products in Rye, New York, was just pushing through the company's revolving door at the end of her day's work when out of nowhere, it seemed, a flustered, worried-sounding woman she'd never seen before popped up alongside her.

"I'm lost," the stranger said. "Altogether lost. I'm a nervous wreck. Can you help me?"

The Avon lady was frightened and hesitated for a split second. It was dark. There was no one around. The woman who had approached her looked haggard, tense. But at once, as if sensing her fear, the stranger explained herself. "I'm a doctor," she said, "from New York. I was on my way to Nantucket, but I started feeling terribly tired a little while ago. I thought I was about to fall asleep at the wheel, so I pulled off the highway. Figured I'd find a hotel and get some sleep." She smiled. "If there's anyone who ought to know better than to drive when exhausted, it's a doctor."

The Avon lady relaxed. The stranger had an amusing, reassuring way of expressing herself and a refined New England accent. When she went on to say "Someone told me there were some places to stay further up this road, but I've been back and forth, back and forth, and haven't seen any," the Avon executive suggested she go to a nearby Marriott hotel, and offered to get into her own car and lead the way.

The lost woman was Margaret Kilcoyne, a New York doctor and medical researcher who, in her own words that night, was "sitting on the Nobel Prize." Two nights later she would become altogether lost—and vanish into thin air from her weekend home on Nantucket Island.

I first learned about the disappearance of Dr. Kilcoyne from the newspapers, and it seemed, from those reports, that she must have committed suicide by drowning herself. Her wallet, passport, bankbook, and summer sandals were found neatly stacked in a pile—the kind of orderly assemblage of personal effects that many suicides make—about a mile inland from the ocean and a half mile from the pond near her home. True, her body hadn't been found. But then, Virginia Woolf's body wasn't discovered until weeks after her suicide. And the bodies of some drowning victims are never found.

I assumed that Dr. Kilcoyne had been depressed and, as a result, had killed herself. Doctors have one of the highest suicide rates in the country. Women doctors, subject to special pressures, may be at even higher risk for self-destruction than their male colleagues. And certainly, from outward appearance, Margaret Kilcoyne, who worked at the Columbia-Presbyterian Medical Center, had had the kind of lonely life that can trigger suicidal depression. Forty-nine years old, she had never married, had no boyfriend, and her principal attachment was to the children of her brother Leo, an executive with IBM, who unfortunately lived far away in Canada. So in February 1980, as I headed for Columbia-Presbyter-

ian to interview some of Kilcoyne's colleagues, I was
certain I would find in their reminiscences the anec-
dotes of lovelessness and despair that have tradition-
ally marked the lives of so many other women
physicians who have brought about their own deaths.
Then, suddenly, I was in the midst of a mystery.

It happened while I was speaking with Dr. Rosa-
mond Kane, a colleague who had know Margaret Kilcoyne for ten years and was, as far as I could
establish, the last person at Columbia to see her.

"What was Margaret Kilcoyne like?" I asked the
white-coated, gray-haired Dr. Kane.

"She was hilarious," Kane said. "She could make the
most mundane subject fascinating. Hyperbole was
her mode of expression. If she started telling you how
she made junket, you'd expect that Vesuvius itself
would rise up on the plate." Then Dr. Kane leaned
forward, troubled, and continued, "That's why I can't
figure this whole thing out. Because it *can't* have
been suicide. Tell me someone has committed suicide
and I'll say, 'Well, yes, maybe he or she was depressed. Or worried about something the rest of us
didn't know about.' But not Margaret."

How could she be so sure? I wanted to know.

"Because not only wasn't Margaret the suicidal
type, but when I saw her, she was particularly bubbly
and excited because she was going on holiday," Dr.
Kane said thoughtfully. "But there's another reason,
too. You see, Margaret was taking penicillin for a superficial skin infection. Well, just before we said
goodbye, she looked in her bag and noticed that she
had only a few pills left. So she asked me to write her
out a new prescription." Dr. Kane leaned forward eagerly. "Do you see? Someone planning to kill herself

wouldn't have been so focused on completing her full course of pills, would she?"

The question hung between us. Certainly, it would seem that if one were contemplating suicide, one wouldn't be worrying about sticking assiduously to the cure for a minor infection.

"Look, I'll tell you something else," Dr. Kane suddenly offered. "One of the things we talked about that afternoon was my gíving her the wheel off my old Volvo, which is the same make as hers. I'd gotten a new car. Margaret wanted the wheel from my old one, and she told me she'd pick it up in four or five days." Dr. Kane shook her head. "I just *know* she wasn't planning to kill herself."

That afternoon I interviewed several other colleagues of Dr. Kilcoyne's. Each one described her much as Dr. Kane had. "She was friendly, outgoing, energetic, and had a marvelous sense of humor," said one research associate, a Dr. Estes. "She was intact, witty, balanced," said another, Dr. Braun. "She was ebullient. That's the best word for her," said Dr. Samuel Ritter, who did clinical work with her. "She was always smiling, and she talked freely, easily, in a stream-of-consciousness kind of fashion, going from one idea to another in a witty, amusing kind of way."

Each of these people had spent time with Dr. Kilcoyne in recent weeks, and because they insisted she hadn't been depressed, I felt the mystery thickening. Still, she could have been secretly in despair, secretly planning to do away with herself, I tried arguing with myself as I entered my home early that evening. The phone was ringing; Dr. Kane was on the other end. "There's one more thing I forgot to tell you," she announced. "Margaret took her ID pin with her to Nantucket. Usually we leave the pins in our lockers. But the nurses were striking at the time, and to enter the building you needed an ID. She took the pin with her—you see?"

I saw. Margaret Kilcoyne, when she left Columbia-Presbyterian on Wednesday, January 23, had every intention of returning to work after the weekend.

I wasn't the only person to discover that Dr. Kilcoyne had clearly been planning to return to her job after her trip to Nantucket, and soon, both on Nantucket and in New York, numerous theories to explain her disappearance began cropping up whenever people discussed it. Primary among them was that the researcher had been the victim of foul play because she'd stumbled on some kind of important scientific discovery. The basis of this supposition lay in the fact that shortly before she disappeared, Margaret Kilcoyne had made a tape recording in which she'd announced that she'd come upon a discovery of Nobel Prize proportion. Her discovery had "the potential for great good to mankind," she'd said, and she herself was shortly going to be "in a position of nationwide power." People who had heard or read about the tape began advancing the notion that she might have been murdered by a jealous colleague or that she had been spirited away by Soviet spies.

Something about these theories got my back up. Those who voiced them struck me as credulous and psychologically unsophisticated. Why assume that just because a person claims to have made a monumental scientific discovery, she in fact has? I made up my mind to try, by finding out as much as I could about Dr. Kilcoyne's research and her final days, to discover why she had disappeared.

What I learned was that although her disappearance *was* mightily mysterious, it wasn't a mystery of cloaks and daggers or murder and mayhem. It was a medical mystery. Margaret Kilcoyne, as all the clues I unearthed began to indicate, had been suffering from a psychiatric disease known to cause sudden disappearances and even sudden accidental deaths. The mystery of her disappearance lay in the disease itself, for while it can easily be detected in the shy, the reserved, the meek, and the depressed, in a person who is naturally cheerful and ebullient, it can so resemble his normal state that even friends and coworkers may not see any problems until it is too late.

The disease is mania, the outstanding features of which are euphoria and hyperactivity. Other signs of the ailment are delusions, particularly those of grandeur, as well as poor judgment and the making of unrealistic decisions.

According to today's most highly respected psychiatric diagnostic tool, the *Diagnostic Statistical Manual III*, drawn up by Columbia-Presbyterian's own Psychiatric Institute, mania has as its essential feature "a distinct period when the predominant mood is either elevated, expansive, or irritable, and when there are the associated symptoms of... hyperactivity, pressure of speech, flight of ideas, inflated self-esteem, decreased need for sleep, distractibility, and excessive involvement in activities with a high potential for painful consequences." The manual advises psychiatrists who interview patients who have possessed for at least one week "at least three" of the above symptoms to make the diagnosis of mania and begin treatment—the favored drug today is lithium—immediately.

Margaret Kilcoyne possessed all seven of the diagnostic symptoms, and her final days were like a living illustration of the manual's definition.

The shift in Margaret Kilcoyne's emotional balance from hypomania, an excited, exuberant state that many of us experience, to mania, an illness, probably started some three weeks before her disappearance. It came as the result of success.

Dr. Kilcoyne had started her career in medicine as a nurse. Then, in the 1950s, she'd decided to go to medical school. Becoming a doctor, she'd taken a position at Columbia-Presbyterian doing clinical research with hypertensive adolescents. But after a few years she found herself yearning to study the brain chemistry involved in hypertension. She was particularly interested in angiotensin II, a peptide that regulates blood pressure. Ian Phillip, a researcher in Iowa, had localized angiotensin II in cells in the hypothalamus, but although others had attempted to replicate his work, no one had succeeded. Dr. Kilcoyne wanted to work on the problem. With all her experience treating the ravages of hypertension in youngsters, she longed to see the disease eradicated. She was convinced that if the peptide regulating blood pressure could be localized, the disease might be conquered.

In 1979, she made up her mind to try to get a grant to do experimental brain research. She'd never done laboratory research before, so in order to get funding she teamed up with an internationally known Columbia neurologist, Dr. Earl Zimmerman. With his guidance, about a year before her disappearance, she submitted a proposal to the National Institutes of Health, outlining her interest in determining which brain cells, if any, contained angiotensin II. To her delight, the NIH agreed to fund the project.

She and Zimmerman began working on angiotensin II in the summer of 1979. It was a happy time for her. She who had been a nurse and managed the unusual step of becoming a doctor had now expanded her horizons even further, entering the heady field of pure research. She began working like a demon, but although she and Zimmerman conducted experiment after experiment, no matter how much they applied themselves, they couldn't find the evasive peptide. Then at last, three weeks before she disappeared, the two researchers triumphed. Angiotensin II *was* present in the brain, they verified, and they could pinpoint the exact spot!

It was a significant scientific discovery, but not as earth-shaking as Dr. Kilcoyne assumed it to be. For her, it was the crown of her career. She was excited, elated, even ecstatic. Zimmerman, used to the ups and downs of academic research, cautioned her against overdramatizing their achievement. "After all," he pointed out, "we weren't the *first*. Phillips was here before us." But she couldn't control her excitement. They'd accomplished something terrifically important, she insisted every time they talked about the discovery. And three days before her disappearance she said to Zimmerman, "Maybe we'll win the Nobel, Earl!"

"Hey, that seems a little strong," he responded. "Maybe now we're going to be able to make some sense of angiotensin II, take it apart, make further experiments, and see where they take us, but right now all we've done is gotten a handle on it."

But Dr. Kilcoyne was not in a mood for caution, and shortly afterward she telephoned her closest relative, her brother Leo in Canada, and told him, "I'm now in a position to win the Nobel Prize" and "I'm in a position of nationwide power." She made a tape recording of the call—a tape recording police found after her disappearance and which sparked the theories that she'd been kidnapped or murdered.

She told her brother during that conversation that her work had "the potential for great good to mankind" but that she was constantly having to buck interference and red tape. She saw the whole situation as a "spiritual test," she said. But no matter. Whatever the stresses, she'd arrived. Her findings were so significant that the other day she'd noticed, just from the way a colleague tilted her head, that she had earned a supreme stature among her peers. She dwelled on this sign of her new status for a while, but then she mentioned an unsettling matter: she was being spied on. Her example: she'd gone into the lab on Sunday, and while she was there the phone had rung; she'd answered it, but there had been no one at the other end of the wire. She'd better go to Nantucket, she told her brother. She'd better get away.

By the end of that conversation, Leo Kilcoyne knew that something was wrong with his sister. Aside from her offering dubious evidence for both grandeur and persecution, her words had been pouring out of her, as if under pressure, and he'd been virtually unable to get a word in edgewise. It was only after considerable effort that at last he was able to say to his sister that since she sounded so overwrought, leaving the city wasn't a bad idea. Indeed, he promised, if she'd go up to Nantucket and take a rest, he'd meet her there on the weekend.

She thanked him, reminding him that he'd previously helped her through a crisis by joining her on the island.

* * *

On Wednesday morning Margaret set out for Nantucket, telling her friends at work that she was exhausted. It wouldn't be the first time that she'd retreated to the island to recover from overwork or overexcitement. She had "heart palpitations," she used to explain, and whenever her heart raced, she would go to the island to calm herself down.

She said goodbye that morning to Dr. Ritter and then to her friend Dr. Kane. She told neither colleague that for several nights running she—like most manics—had had no more than an hour or two of sleep. Nor did she mention that she believed herself to be on the verge of winning the Nobel Prize. She saved both those telling pieces of information for a stranger, the young Avon executive she encountered in Rye. Indeed, the Avon lady learned quite a lot about Margaret Kilcoyne that night, for once they got to the Marriott, the doctor decided that perhaps it was dinner, not sleep, that she needed, and the two women proceeded to eat, drink and chat for hours.

The woman from Avon found Margaret Kilcoyne fascinating. "I'd never met anyone quite so knowledgeable before," she told me, "or so compelling." She and Dr. Kilcoyne discussed many things—not just science but politics, music, food, and wine, although, in classic manic style, Dr. Kilcoyne did most of the talking. Her quick mind ranged swiftly from subject to subject, idea to idea. And, true to type, she ordered munificently. Few things characterize manics more than their tendency toward economic expansiveness, and sitting in the Marriott, where the cuisine hardly warranted the gesture, Margaret Kilcoyne asked for, and managed to obtain, a bottle of Lafite-Rothschild 1970.

Much later in the evening, she made friends with the waitress who served the wine and ended by offering the young woman, who acknowledged that she'd studied psychology in college, a job. She would shortly be setting up a lab on Nantucket, Dr. Kilcoyne explained, and the waitress could be one of the first of the many employees she was planning to have.

By the time the meal was finished, it was one in the morning and all the rooms at the Marriott were filled. The Avon lady generously offered to put up her new friend at her house for the night, and the two women went to her home and to bed. But at five-thirty in the morning, the cosmetics executive suddenly awakened and, getting out of bed, looked into Dr. Kilcoyne's room. Her guest, she noticed with surprise, was up and gone already, despite her earlier insistence on needing sleep. She was worried, but an hour later she received a reassuring call from the doctor, who explained that since she hadn't been able to sleep more than an hour or two, she'd decided to get an early start.

Up to this point, Margaret Kilcoyne had hidden her mania from her colleagues, revealing it only in front of strangers, people who couldn't recognize it because they had no basis of comparison. But when she arrived on Nantucket on Friday, January 25, her mania began to be apparent to people who knew her. Shopping, she spent $650 in just a few minutes, buying groceries in multiples of three and explaining to the A&P clerks that she needed vast quantities of food because she'd soon be holding a press conference and crowds of reporters would be there. To the cab driver who drove her and the supplies home, she said that after her press conference, she'd be establishing a major scientific lab on Nantucket.

That night she had dinner with friends, Grace and Richard Coffin, and with her brother, who, true to his word, had arrived on the island. The Coffins and Leo knew Margaret was out of control. She barely stopped talking throughout the evening, and the Coffins, who wanted to tell Leo about their recent trip to Mexico, had to beg her to be quiet. When they did, she at last decided that she'd best go to bed. In the morning, when Leo went to awaken her at six forty-five, she had vanished.

What could have happened to Margaret Kilcoyne? I finally concluded, and her family concurred with me, that in her manic, delusional state she could have acted on almost any mad, grandiose notion. She could have believed, for example, that she could take a little dip in the January ocean without getting chilled or even that she could walk on water. Most likely these thoughts didn't occur to her when she first left her house. She must have left hurriedly, for she didn't take a coat, but she must have been worried, for she did take her passport and wallet. Perhaps she was once again imagining that someone was trying to steal her research and thus had made up her mind to flee. But where? How? Perhaps it was then that the idea of fleeing over water occurred to her. She piled up her possessions. And then she must have taken wing, must, with the notorious bad judgment of manics, have accidentally drowned herself. It was suicide, although not the usual kind of suicide, which is death by despair. It was death by delusion.

DENTED PRIDE

New York, New York

1983

On a street corner in Manhattan's SoHo district one warm September evening, an aged, clunky 1964 Chevy station wagon dented the rear of a new red Ferrari. The Ferrari was driven by Frank Magliato, the thirty-two-year-old owner of a fashionable SoHo boutique. A twenty-four-year-old New Jersey man named Anthony Giani, who had come to the city to buy drugs, was riding in the Chevy. Before the night was out, the businessman would go home, get a gun, and shoot the visitor from New Jersey right above the eye.

Men have often taken up arms to avenge an injury to their country, their home, their family, but this seemed to be something new—an act of rage for injuries inflicted on an automobile. Giani died in a hospital three days later. Magliato was put on trial and convicted of homicide.

He had led an apparently exemplary life until the day of the incident, whereas his victim had been a violent, depraved man. Their encounter, and Magliato's fate, raised age-old questions of morality and justice.

In August 1983, a month before the two men met, Anthony Giani's life had started to whirl to pieces. It had been coming apart slowly for several years, ever since 1975. He'd been sixteen then, a slim, average-size young fellow without any particular ambition. He dropped out of high school that year and started working, taking a variety of jobs. For a while he was an elevator operator, then a cab driver, then a cab dispatcher, then a factory worker. Nothing lasted. When he was eighteen, he began using heroin.

His mother, Rosemarie Giani, blamed in part the hardness of her life when Anthony was little. She and his father, Anthony Giani, Sr., of Jersey City, New Jersey, had three children in quick succession: Anthony first, then two girls, Donna and Michelle. But shortly after Michelle was born—Anthony was six—the Gianis split up and Mrs. Giani went to work to support her three youngsters. Commuting to her job as a secretary in a financial company, she left the children in good hands, those of their grandmother. But the older woman was getting on in years, and dealing with three little ones wasn't easy, particularly since Michelle was brain-damaged and needed constant attention. The other two children may have gotten short shrift. But what was worst for the family, Mrs. Giani felt, was that they were always on the move. Her salary was small. She couldn't afford to buy a home, so she rented. But it seemed, she told me, "as if whenever we'd get settled and live in a house for a year, the owners would decide to sell, and we'd be out looking again."

Still, the Gianis got by. Holding on to the same job for sixteen years, Rosemarie ultimately managed to afford a special private school for Michelle and to send Donna to college. But Anthony became more and more of a problem.

He kept getting arrested—in 1979, for receiving stolen property; in 1980, for burglary and theft; in

1981, for lying drunk on a street. Later in 1981 he was arrested several more times—for having a concealed knife, for stealing a CB radio, for ripping up a traffic ticket. In some cases, the charges were dismissed; in others, he was convicted and had to pay fines.

He also kept getting into fights. When a cab driver complained that he'd failed to pay for a ride, he battered the cab. When a man accidentally shoved aside his girlfriend as she stood at a bar, he attacked the man. Worst of all, according to a probation report, he beat his brain-damaged sister.

His temper was terrifying. One former girlfriend told an investigator that even when he wasn't high on drugs, "he would have tantrums and fits of anger. He'd cry or plead or bang his head against the wall, lie on the floor and kick his feet, or pull out his hair." She recalled going with him once to Union Square in Manhattan, where he tried to buy drugs. When some dealers attempted to rip him off, he "became crazed, began screaming and pushing them around. Guns went off in the air, and he kept right on fighting and arguing." When he was high on drugs, his tantrums were even stranger. "One night, I was at Anthony's house," the girlfriend said, "and all of a sudden he got real angry and started spitting at the TV, which was turned off. . . . I became very frightened and wanted to leave, but he wouldn't let me. I got more scared and had to lock myself in the bathroom to protect myself. He was banging on the door, and if he got to me, I'm sure he would have hurt me."

That was in 1981. By 1983 Giani was, if anything, even more out of control. He was arrested for stealing in February, March, and early August. After the last arrest, he was sent to a medical center for a psychiatric evaluation. But a few days later, on August 9, he slipped away from the hospital for the night. The next day, he returned with two bags of marijuana hidden in his shoes. The drugs were discovered and he was arrested again. It was his twenty-fourth birthday.

Perhaps it was because he had started his twenty-fifth year with an arrest, or perhaps it was because he had twice lost consciousness while on drugs, but on Friday, September 2, Giani made an effort to change his life. He presented himself to a methadone clinic in Jersey City and was admitted to its twenty-one-day drug detoxification program. Trying to be cooperative with his interviewer, he told as much about himself as he could find to say, explaining that he had been thrown out of his home, that he was living from day to day with friends, that he had no social life, no recreational activities, "no outlet besides going to movies."

He also admitted that he had a $40- to $80-a-day heroin habit and that he was using cocaine about five times a week. A test of his body fluids drawn that day revealed traces of morphine and quinine in his system.

That there are men like Anthony Giani on the streets of big cities is a fact that affects the lives of all city-dwellers, causing them daily to have to moderate their movements, regulate their responses. Men like Frank Magliato are another story, the Horatio Algers of our times, the climbers, the winners, the symbols of the vitality of our metropolises, where fortunes can still be made in one generation by those shrewd and industrious enough to apply themselves. Consider the contrast. At the very time Anthony Giani was being given his urine test for drugs in New Jersey, Frank

Magliato was starting his Labor Day weekend at his summer rental in fashionable Southampton. His girlfriend, a jewelry designer, was visiting her parents in Florida that weekend, so for company he had brought along his dog, a costly Shar-Pei.

He needed the holiday. He'd been working hard, both at Diddingtons, the SoHo boutique of which he was the principal owner, and at a relatively new career: stockbroking. The year before, he'd obtained a license and begun brokering part time. Very soon afterward, he had become president and part owner of E.C. Farnsworth & Company, a small brokerage firm. His had been a phenomenal rise.

He'd grown up in Farmingdale, Long Island, the oldest son of a photoengraver. His father's brothers, too, were blue-collar workers—one a trucker, the other a horse trainer at a racetrack. But Frank and *his* brothers—there were three boys altogether—quickly entered the ranks of the middle class. One of his brothers became prominent in the insurance business; the other, president of Frank's business, Diddingtons.

As a youth, Frank hadn't anticipated having a business of his own. He'd attended a technical college, Rensselaer Polytechnic Institute in Troy, New York, and worked during his summer vacations at whatever came to hand—first in a sunglass factory, later at a Korvette's in Albany, where he started as a janitor and rose to salesman. But he was bright and ambitious, and after graduating in 1973, he took a job in the field he had studied, environmental engineering, and within a couple of years was developing plans for fossil-fuel power plants for the New York Power Authority. He was doing well in his chosen profession, but around that time he realized he wanted something more out of life, wanted to run something, to be his own boss. In 1978, still only in his twenties, he opened a small clothing boutique in Greenwich Village called Diddingtons, a venture he went into with a girlfriend. Magliato proved himself a talented entrepreneur: Diddingtons was a brilliant success. A year later, the shop moved to a far larger, far more promising location in SoHo.

Soon Magliato began seeking even newer horizons, new challenges. He bought real estate—a two-bedroom duplex co-op, a one-seventh share in a valuable building in the Village, and part of the Diddingtons building. He invested in a stylish restaurant. And he started brokering. In all his ventures he was successful.

His relatives considered him not only hard-working and clever but thoughtful and generous. He'd give them free financial advice, lend them clothes from his shops when they had nothing to wear to important interviews or appointments. He nursed his mother through a lengthy terminal illness. "He was gentle and considerate," his brother Joseph told me.

But not everyone thought so highly of him. One neighbor in his Village co-op said, "He could be sharp. Self-centered. Once, a woman here objected to the fact that he would let his dog run around the lobby without a leash, and when she complained, he told her, 'When you leash your child, I'll leash my dog.'"

Still, there was little about him to suggest that he could ever be a killer. He wasn't prone to sudden bursts of temper, wasn't a bully or a brawler. When the police investigated his past to see if he had previously gotten himself into explosive situations, they came up empty-handed. And virtually all his friends described him as uncommonly good-natured. "He had the sweetest disposition," one female friend said. "He was very level-headed, not at all the type who'd get excited or irritable in a crisis," said another. "He has such a relaxed view of the many complications of life that it is a joy to be with him," said a third.

I myself, interviewing him on several occasions during his trial, found his temperament remarkably cheerful. He kept reassuring me that everything would work out all right because "I have truth on my side." Interestingly, however, his unusually optimistic nature may have had a great deal to do with what happened to him in SoHo on the night his car was dented. It may have been the very thing that caused him to engage in a series of escalating confrontations with Anthony Giani, a man from whom most other people would have beat a swift retreat.

Or perhaps it was just that he had a weapon. He was licensed to own two guns. One was a .38-caliber detective special. The other, an elaborate automatic, was a 9-mm Walther. He bought the first, he told me, because he often carried large sums of money from Diddingtons to the bank. "I had thirteen female employees working for me," he explained. "I felt I needed the gun to protect not just myself but them."

He bought the second gun, a German police weapon, because a shopkeeper urged it on him as a collector's item. Magliato liked objects. He collected Clarice Cliff pottery, old postcards, early slot machines, antique furniture. So he bought the fancy weapon and applied for a second gun license, this time getting a permit that limited use of the gun to target practice.

He never used it, though. It remained in its box, neat and clean. He rarely shot the .38, either. After searching the records of various shooting ranges, the police discovered that the young businessman had signed in for practice only three or four times and, in all, had had only about fifteen minutes' training.

At about the same time he bought his guns, Magliato got a Mercedes, leasing it from a rental company and charging it as a business expense to a consulting firm he had set up. He had always liked cars, particularly expensive European models and sports cars. His first car, bought when he was eighteen, had been a Karmann Ghia. At twenty-one, he got an 850 Fiat Spider; at twenty-four, a 124 Fiat Sports Spider. Later, he got the Mercedes. Then, in March 1983, he decided to go all the way. He leased a new Ferrari, paying $18,000 down and a monthly fee of $525. At the time, there were fewer than fifteen thousand in the United States. Magliato decided to get his in red.

He took good care of his prized auto. When he parked it in his garage, he covered it with a big plastic sheet. And he arranged to park it himself so it wouldn't be exposed to the careless handling of attendants.

On the Tuesday after Labor Day, Magliato drove the Ferrari proudly, with its top down, from Southampton to Manhattan. Soo Ling, the Shar-Pei, was with him, and he had another passenger as well, seventeen-year-old Eddie Klaris, the son of a lawyer friend who'd had to return to Manhattan the day before and so couldn't drive his boy home. Magliato had offered Klaris—a student at the Dwight School, a private high school—a lift into town.

Meanwhile, Anthony Giani, too, had been given a lift into town by his friend Donald Schneider. With Schneider at the wheel of his Chevy station wagon, the two left Jersey City in the early evening and went to Washington Square Park. On the way, they brought some marijuana.

The red Ferrari reached the Village at about 8 P.M. Magliato drove first to his apartment, dropping off his clothes and the dog. Then he told Klaris that he'd take him home after he stopped at Diddingtons, nearby, to check on the day's receipts and pick up some money. But as they drove west the Ferrari was suddenly struck from behind by the station wagon. A moment later, the Chevy sped away.

Impulsively, without getting out to inspect for any damage, Magliato took off after the wagon. He was indignant about the accident and about the Chevy's abrupt departure. "I'll get them, I'll kill them," he told Klaris. He meant the words as a figure of speech, he later insisted.

Magliato followed the Chevy as it sped west, then south. At one corner, both cars got stuck at a red light, and Magliato started to get out. He later said he was going to demand that the driver of the Chevy give him his car registration and insurance cards. But now Anthony Giani sprang out of the Chevy on the passenger side, shouting and holding a heavy-looking club. Eddie Klaris reached down among his possessions and handed Magliato a tennis racquet, saying, "Here, you might need this." But Magliato had changed his mind about approaching the driver. Giani looked ominous. He was disheveled, his eyes were wild and glazed, and he was waving the club in the air, screaming, "Get out of here, mother——."

His heart pounding, Magliato got back into the Ferrari. But he didn't abandon the chase. The Chevy sped away, this time leaving Giani in the street, and Magliato took off after it. He followed it as it turned left for a while, then right, and all the time Klaris kept trying to make out the license plate. Suddenly, they were back at the corner where Magliato had started to get out of his car, and there was Giani, still standing in the street. The businessman pointed the front end of the Ferrari right at the loiterer, then swerved past. He later said he had to force Giani to jump back because, with the top of the Ferrari down, Giani could have smacked Klaris on the head with the club. Schneider, who had parked the Chevy, got a different impression. He telephoned the police, reporting that someone in a red sports car was trying to run down his friend.

By this time, Klaris had seen the Chevy's license plate number, and he suggested that they give up the chase and report everything to the police. Magliato seemed to concur. He began driving around SoHo, ostensibly looking for a cop. None was in sight. But they saw the Chevy again, at least according to Klaris. Unoccupied, it was parked at Broome and West Broadway, he said. (And he later told police that it was Magliato who first spotted it, saying, "Hey, there's the car!")

Their search for a policeman in SoHo so far unsuccessful, Klaris suggested that they might find a policeman in the Village. His father lived there, and he'd often noticed cops stationed at the arch in Washington Square Park. Magliato concurred and headed uptown, and the two of them peered into the park, but they didn't see any cops. "You can never find one when you need one," they told each other.

A few minutes later, Magliato told Klaris that instead of looking any further, they should go straight to a station house. But first, he said, they ought to stop at his apartment. He'd left his driver's license in his wallet when he'd dropped off his clothes, and he didn't want to talk to the police without it.

Klaris waited in the car in front of the business-man's apartment building while he hurried upstairs. He was gone five minutes. When he returned, he had his license and his wallet—and his .38. He told Klaris, who was worried about the gun, that he'd brought it for protection, in case on their way to the police they came across the men from the Chevy. Once, he added, when some people had threatened him, he'd pulled out his gun and they'd disappeared, just like that. (Although on the night of the killing Magliato seemed to display the sort of impulsive be-havior often engaged in by people on cocaine, he told me he had never taken drugs.)

Shortly afterward, while driving downtown toward the First Police Precinct, Magliato and Klaris passed the corner of Broome and West Broadway. There, just where they'd seen it before, was the parked Chevy. Magliato pulled over and got out of the Ferrari, the gun in his waistband. The occupants of the Chevy were nowhere in sight. At last, Magliato directed Klaris to call the police.

The boy ran to a corner phone booth, dialed 911, and began reporting the accident when, suddenly, he saw Giani and Schneider standing across the street. They saw him and Magliato, and a moment later, Giani went to the Chevy, reached inside, and got out his club. Magliato took the gun from the waistband. He struck a combat stance, his arms extended, and cocked the weapon. A shot echoed in the street. At once, Giani was sprawled on the ground.

Klaris hung up the phone. Giani had been hit, from a distance of about forty feet, just above his right eye.

* * *

The corner of Broome and West Broadway erupted into pandemonium. The shooting had occurred right in front of a popular hangout, the Broome Street Bar, and there were many people on the street. A young clothing designer had been sitting on a stoop with a friend, not far from Giani. When Magliato raised his gun, she found herself looking right at the barrel. "I sat there frozen. I didn't take my eyes off it," she said. When the gun went off, she bolted hysterically, racing a third of the way down the block before returning to the gathering crowd.

Not just the shooting but the start of the fight had been witnessed by several people. It had begun, these witnesses later told police, when someone—either Giani or Magliato—had shouted out, "Hey, f——, come here! I've been looking for you!" But the witnesses were confused about which man had thrown down the gauntlet. One woman who'd overheard the taunt thought the man with the club had made it, while another wasn't at all sure and said it could have been the man with the gun. But whoever had said it, she insisted, the other had promptly yelled back, "Oh, yeah?"

There was also some confusion about who had raised his weapon first. One woman was sure it had been the man with the club. Several were certain it was the man with the gun and that the man with the club hadn't ever even lifted his at all. The police took down all these accounts and scanned the crowd for the gunman. But by that time he had vanished.

He had gone home, taking Klaris with him. The boy thought they should have waited and talked to the police and told him this, but Magliato, although shaken, insisted there was no point. The whole thing would just blow over, the police would probably think it was some kind of drug shootout, he said optimistically. They'd never connect it to him.

Klaris was dubious. He'd had to give the cops his name when he'd called 911, he reminded Magliato. The businessman said not to worry: "They probably got it down wrong." Still, Klaris thought they should go to the police, and he kept pleading until at last Magliato agreed. They'd go. But not now, he said. Not until the next day, when he could appear in a suit and tie, not in the jeans and T-shirt he was wearing.

Magliato never did go to the police, and two days later the police located Klaris. They had telephoned his mother's house, and his brother had told them Eddie was at his father's home in the Village. As it turned out, he was there with Magliato; the two of them were setting up a stereo system. Magliato had made the boy promise not to say a thing to anybody about the incident, not even to his parents, and Klaris had kept his word. But now, learning through a telephone call from his brother that the police were on their way, he panicked. So did Magliato, who left abruptly, pausing at the door just long enough to gesture at Klaris in sign language. According to the student, the older man put a finger to his lips, then drew it across his throat.

But Klaris did talk, and three weeks later Magliato was indicted for the murder of Giani.

The trial began in New York State Supreme Court on September 17, 1984, just over a year after the date of the shooting. Many of Magliato's friends attended, and several of them spoke privately about what they saw as the unfairness of trying an upstanding man like Magliato for the death of an outcast like Giani. They had learned about Giani's past and felt that in some way his life hardly counted. One man, a well-known journalist, told me, "Giani was what my mother used to call *sgutsim*. Trash. So he's dead. So what's the fuss all about?" Another said, "Frank did society a service."

Murder trials, however, are not about the crimes of the victim but about the possible crimes of the defendant. The jury would not be told about Giani's past, only about what had transpired when Giani and Magliato met. "In our society," the presiding judge, Thomas R. Sullivan, later explained eloquently, "there are no castes, no outlaws, no classes of people who are pariahs, no one who, no matter his lifestyle or past transgressions, becomes fair game. Life cannot be *forfeited*."

Magliato had hired Gerald Lefcourt, one of New York's most able young criminal lawyers, to defend him. In 1971, Lefcourt had successfully defended thirteen Black Panthers. In 1974, he had won an acquittal for Henry Brown, a man accused of killing two New York policemen for the Black Liberation Army. Lefcourt had also represented Yippi Abbie Hoffman, and he had helped defend the Chicago 7, the antiwar activists charged with conspiracy at the 1968 Democratic National Convention. In brief, he was a man with a keen interest in the social issues involved in the law.

So, too, was the prosecutor, Assistant District Attorney John Lenoir. A lawyer for only five years, Lenoir had spent most of his professional life as an anthropologist, earning a Ph.D. and living for three years in a tribal village in Suriname. There he became interested in the law after watching how primitive cultures resolved disputes. In the hands of these two men, the case of the red Ferrari emerged as a sharp sociological drama. To Lefcourt, Magliato was Everyman, beset on all sides by crime and violence, persecuted if he tried to defend himself. To Lenoir, Magliato was the classic vigilante, the man who takes justice into his own hands and who, though a hero in modern movies, is as much a menace to society as are the evils he seeks to correct.

The prosecution relied chiefly on the eyewitnesses from SoHo and on Eddie Klaris, who had come down from his first year at Vassar for the trial. Klaris seemed to quiver on the stand, perhaps torn between some lingering loyalty to Magliato and the damning account he was giving. It was damning indeed, for the boy insisted that they had obtained the Chevy's license number and had seen where the car was parked well before Magliato got his gun—testimony that was ultimately critical for the jury.

The defense relied chiefly on Magliato's own testimony. In almost a full day on the witness stand, he told the story of his life before the confrontation with Giani. As for that fatal meeting, he insisted that the shooting was an accident. When he drew and cocked the weapon, it was only to keep Giani covered until the police arrived. But he grew so rattled that the gun went off on its own. "I didn't mean to pull the trigger," he said.

The defense also produced character witnesses and a chilling triumvirate of gun experts, one of them a graduate of Yale University and Harvard Law School. The experts contended that guns like Magliato's could fire accidentally, particularly if the shooter was under stress. The three bore a striking resemblance to one another. Each sported a bushy mustache, as if it were a trademark. Two had attended Soldier of Fortune conventions. Among them, they had written over a thousand articles, with such titles as "Buckshot Breakthrough," "Shooting Through Coat Pockets," and "Hit the White Part," for magazines like *S.W.A.T., Gun World*, and *Gun Digest*. They thought the fact that Magliato had managed to hit Giani right above the eyes from a distance of about forty feet was just beginner's luck—or misfortune.

Throughout the trial, Magliato seemed certain of vindication. During breaks, he made small talk with his family and friends, asking about an aunt's sore foot, a friend's problem at work. He was free on $1 million bond, and each evening he hurried off with his companions, loping along in his awkward, gangly manner.

Giani's mother was there every day, too. All day she clutched a crucifix, and she told me that whenever the talk turned to weapons, she looked down at the crucifix and thought to herself, *This* is *my* weapon. Once, she turned to her lawyer and said it aloud.

At last, after three weeks of testimony, the trial drew to a close and the lawyers gave their summations. First, the defense: Magliato had picked up his gun out of fear, and Giani had died as the result of a "tragic freak accident." Then the prosecution: Magliato had shown a "depraved indifference to human life" by pulling the trigger on a crowded street, and he'd shot Giani not because he had "dented his car but because Giani had dented his pride."

The judge's instructions were complicated. The jury could convict Magliato of any of five crimes—or none at all. There were two separate counts of murder in the second degree: intentional murder and so-called depraved murder, murder resulting from a reckless indifference to human life. There were two counts of manslaughter: manslaughter one, an intentional act, and manslaughter two, a reckless act. And there was one count not bearing a mandatory jail sentence: criminally negligent homicide.

The jurors deliberated for two days, repeatedly asking the judge to reread his instructions. They also asked at one point whether certain of the charges were more serious than others. The judge, telling them to decide which crime, if any, the evidence seemed to support, warned them that they were not supposed to think about punishment, for such is New York law. The defense objected to this warning, suspecting that the jury might be trying to convict Magliato of one of the less serious crimes.

In the middle of the second day of deliberations, after hearing the charges for a fourth time, the jury finally pronounced Magliato guilty of depraved murder. His girlfriend, the jewelry designer, wept copiously. Mrs. Giani's fingers caressed her crucifix. And Magliato shuddered. Then, SoHo and Southampton suddenly behind him, he was abruptly swept off to jail by a phalanx of guards.

I visited him at Riker's Island two weeks later. He was again cheerful and optimistic. His luck had turned, he told me. His lawyer had received from Judge Sullivan a copy of a remarkable letter. One of the jurors, a woman, had wirtten to the judge, spelling out in great detail a conflict that had come up in the jury room. The conflict turned out to be precisely what Lefcourt had suspected. The jurors had been trying to compromise, to convict Magliato of one of the lesser crimes, but they hadn't understood how to go about it. According to the letter, they had screened out intentional murder and were deadlocked on intentional manslaughter. At this point, the woman wrote, she and several other jurors had concluded that depraved murder might be a less serious offense than intentional manslaughter because it appeared third on their verdict sheet, so they had voted for this crime.

There were other confusions, she said—about the meaning of "depraved" and about the difference between murder and manslaughter. "I admit to you your Honor that we do not appear to be very bright," the juror wrote. But she begged Judge Sullivan to review what had happened because she thought that Magliato had been denied his right to a fair trial.

Another juror had sent Magliato a poem. And a third had telephoned Lefcourt and confirmed the account of confusion in the jury room. So Magliato was exuberant. And, surprisingly, he hadn't been having a bad time at Riker's, he told me. He'd been sleeping and eating well and had been reading *The Grapes of Wrath* and rereading *War and Peace*. He'd also been getting a kick out of observing his fellow inmates. "Would you believe," he asked, "that none of the guys here were interested in watching the vice-presidential debate? There are two TV sets, and everyone votes about what to watch. There were only two votes for the debate, so everyone watched some murder movie instead."

Then, obviously a sharp student of value structures, he began to describe the new world he had been forced to enter. "It's like a great big fraternity house," he said. "Only what you have in common isn't sports or classes but criminal stuff, like whether you're here 'on a body.' Some people have one body, some two, some none. I've got one, so that lends me a certain distinction."

Did he miss anything?

"Friends," he said. And he also told me that he thought the make of his car had a great deal to do with everything that had happened to him. He said that if he hadn't been driving a Ferrari, Giani and Schneider might never have hit him in the first place and that the police, the D.A.'s office, and even the judicial system might have been less harsh on him, perhaps letting him plead guilty to criminally negligent homicide. There is something symbolic about a Ferrari, he maintained, something that arouses prejudices in others. What bothered him most about this fact was, he said, that his "wasn't even one of those eighty-thousand-dollar Ferraris. It was a special European car, only a thirty-nine-thousand-dollar model."

His friends were all in court on the day of his sentencing. Surprisingly, so were four jurors—three regulars, one alternate. The jurors had come to demonstrate their concern about the verdict. They sat together in a back row, exchanging reminiscences and copies of their protests and poetry.

The woman who had written to Judge Sullivan told me, "I've done what I did as a matter of conscience." An administrative assistant at a law firm, she belonged to a theater group and owned a horse. "I blame myself for not speaking up in the jury room," she said. "But I felt intimidated, because there were outbursts when some of us wanted to reopen deliberations. There were people in there who just wanted to go home."

The jurors' afterthoughts had little effect on the day's proceedings. Judge Sullivan declared that he'd found this particularly troublesome, largely because some of the blame for Giani's death rested on the community. "We require of policemen who get guns that they have at least ten hours of training in how to handle their weapons," he said. "But we let any ordinary citizen who shows need of a gun get one, and then we don't demand that he learn safety and competency. By Magliato's own testimony, he had only fifteen minutes' training with the gun." Then, taking Magliato's previously unsullied record into consideration, Sullivan sentenced him to the minimum for murder—fifteen years to life (the maximum would have been twenty-five to life).

A year later, while Magliato was serving time in an upstate New York jail, an appellate court reduced his crime from murder to manslaughter. He had been guilty, in the view of three judges on the five-person court, not of a "depraved indifference to human life," but of having caused a death through recklessness. The businessman was joyous, according to his lawyer, Lefcourt, and was anticipating that he might be freed on probation. No doubt, in his inimitable, optimistic way, he may have even begun to make plans for a rosy future. But at a resentencing hearing, Judge Sullivan, saying, "Nothing new has been presented to me. A man was killed who did not deserve to die," again confined him to jail, this time for a term of four to twelve years for manslaughter.

It was a crushing blow for Magliato, who seemed stunned and perplexed. But I thought of Nietzsche, who warned, "Whoever fights monsters should see to it that in the process he does not become a monster." In the space of a few crucial moments on a late summer evening, Magliato had jeopardized all he had gained in his lifetime by becoming as reckless, as monstrous, if you will, as the man who was his victim.

DR. QUAALUDE

New York, New York

1979

In the Spring of 1977, Richard Macris, a nineteen-year-old student at New York University, became an assistant in the laboratory of Dr. John Buettner-Janusch, chairman of the Anthropology Department. For the young undergraduate, the appointment was a coup. To be singled out to work in the anthropology chairman's lab meant that he had passed a tougher test than any written exam. Buettner-Janusch was famous for smiling on only the best and the brightest.

Macris began his work—centrifuging and analyzing blood samples—eagerly. Buettner-Janusch had made his name, some years earlier, by doing complex biological studies that had established relationships between the blood proteins of lemurs and those of the higher anthropoids, and Macris was under the impression that the experiments he was being asked to do were somehow related to the chairman's interest in monkey-to-man blood factor.

Buettner-Janusch had come to NYU in 1973. His academic credentials were impeccable. He'd received a B.A., B.S., and M.A. from the University of Chicago and a Ph.D. from the University of Michigan. He'd taught at Yale for seven years and in that time written a highly regarded anthropology textbook, *The Origins of Man*. Then he'd moved to Duke University in

North Carolina, where he'd gone on to do elegant research into the blood relationships among lemurs, apes, and man, research that answered key questions about evolution. By 1973, the forty-nine-year-old Buettner-Janusch was one of the best-known physical anthropologists not just in the United States but in the world, and he regularly received large research grants from the National Science Foundation. Indeed, he was so respected a scholar that NYU had to lure him away from Duke by promising him a new and lavish research facility, which cost the university $200,000.

Macris, a middle-class youth from Queens whose Greek Orthodox family had had to make sacrifices to send him to college, felt fortunate indeed throughout his first days in the costly facility. With lab experience, he would surely be able to get into graduate school, perhaps even win a good fellowship. But shortly after he began his work, he heard disturbing rumors. Some of the other lab assistants, boastful about their old-timer status and close relationships with Buettner-Janusch, hinted that B-J, as they fondly called him, wasn't doing lemur research at all; he was making illegal drugs—methaqualone and LSD. One day, one of the old-timers told Macris to wash his hands carefully because the material he was handling "could cause you to go crazy."

Macris didn't quite believe the rumors. Still, there *were* funny things about the lab. As time went on, he noticed that former students of the chairman's, fellows who had long since graduated, were turning up in the lab. They arrived at odd hours, often at night, and held whispered conversations with B-J. Then, one day B-J asked him to come in on a Saturday, and when he got there, the chairman closed all the doors to the customarily unguarded facility and indicated that today they would be making anacetyl anthranilic acid, a precursor of LSD.

From that time forward, Macris began to wonder if the stories he'd heard could be true, and in early February 1979 he confronted B-J with his suspicions.

The chairman shrugged them off. "We're making neurotoxins to be used with lemurs," he said.

"Isn't it available commercially?" Macris asked.

"Yes," the chairman answered, "but the commercial product isn't pure enough."

Macris's conscience started to bother him. Suppose the chairman *was* making illegal drugs. Suppose they weren't for use with lab animals. Perhaps he ought to notify the school authorities. Troubled, he sought the counsel of another renowned NYU professor, Dr. Clifford Jolly, an anthropologist who worked in the lab next door.

Jolly listened to Macris's suspicions, then warned him that he was making a weighty charge. If what he was suggesting was true, Buettner-Janusch was breaking the law and could get into serious trouble. But if the boy reported his suspicions and there was no truth to the charge, he himself would be in serious trouble. Jolly advised him to keep his anxieties to himself but to start keeping a notebook of all experiments being conducted in the lab. And, said Jolly, he himself would see what he could find out.

Professor Jolly, an Englishman, had been an admirer of Buettner-Janusch and had even served on the search committee that had brought him to NYU. He respected the chairman, but he too had had misgivings about him for some time. He couldn't quite put his finger on why, except that there was about the chairman a breath of the outrageous, an air of *épater le bourgeoisie*. And once B-J had said something peculiar to him. It was back in the winter of 1978, when the National Science Foundation had unexpectedly turned down his grant request. B-J had said to Jolly that he wasn't worried about this rejection because there was a possibility of finding alternative funds for the lab. He might get money from private foundations—and other sources. When Jolly had thought about what these might be, unaccountably, he'd been scared. But he'd put the conversation out of his mind until the day Richard Macris came to him.

In the next few months, Jolly began acting like an amateur sleuth. At night, when the student assistants had all gone home, he snapped photographs of their equipment and sifted through notes in their wastebaskets. Every two weeks, he took samples from chemical flasks and vials in the lab and stored them in a bookcase in his home. One day he submitted these samples to the federal Drug Enforcement Agency and soon afterward, the DEA, without knowing where or by whom the chemicals had been made, reported back that one sample was methaqualone—known as Quaalude—an illegal drug.

What was he to do? Professor Jolly got in touch with Richard Macris and the two went at once to John C. Sawhill, then NYU's president, and told him what they'd discovered. Sawhill informed the U.S. Attorney's office, and the following night, without a search warrant but with the authorization of NYU, DEA agents surreptitiously searched the anthropology lab, seizing various pieces of equipment and numerous chemicals.

The chemicals were analyzed and found to contain LSD, methaqualone, and synthetic cocaine, and almost immediately the government opened a full-scale but secret investigation of Buettner-Janusch. The detectives would be a handful of junior gumshoes—students who, like Macris, were working in the lab. Some were persuaded, and some volunteered, to monitor B-J's correspondence, to listen in on his conversations, and even to wear hidden tape recorders on their bodies when they spoke to him.

At first Buettner-Janusch didn't know he was being investigated. On the night of the search, Macris and Jolly had let the agents into the lab with a key, but the search party had, upon leaving, broken down the frame of the lab door in order to make their visit appear to be a burglary. The chairman had been merely irritated at the time. But quite quickly he began to suspect that the burglary hadn't been haphazard, for six days later he remarked to Macris, "I've been denounced by someone. But who? Who?" And he said to a student named Danny Cornyetz, the director of the lab, "The only thing that's missing is, who's the goddamn informant?"

It would have been intolerable to him to suspect that his student assistants, the very people he had rewarded with his favors and power, could be disloyal. He was a man who insisted on loyalty, running his department in so authoritarian, so dictatorial a way that he even expected students who sought advancement from him to make his enemies theirs. And for the most part his students complied. "We were discouraged from taking courses with any of the professors of whom B-J disapproved," one student explained to me. "And we accepted this, believing that if we wanted to study the subject matter any of these professors taught, and went ahead and registered for their classes despite the warnings, we wouldn't get recommended for graduate school, or we might even get flunked out. Lots of us just went along with this. And it got so bad that one of the professors B-J didn't like, a man who had a specially endowed chair in the department and ten thousand dollars' worth of fellowship money to give away every year, couldn't even find any student takers for his money."

It was hardly the ideal academic atmosphere. But then B-J was hardly the typical academic.

Showy and sartorially splendid, he dyed his graying hair blond and dressed in expensive suits and custom-tailored shirts. He enjoyed the opera and ballet and went frequently to the Met. His spacious apartment on Washington Square was decorated with exquisite Navajo rugs and the finest American Indian pottery. His wife of many years, Vina Mallowitz, a biochemist, had died in 1977, but he had a wide circle of friends—not just scholars but playwrights and novelists and painters—and took great pleasure in entertaining them lavishly. His large parties were gala affairs, catered and served by uniformed butlers and maids. His small ones features costly wines and gourmet fare that he himself cooked.

But if living well was one of his favorite pursuits, shocking people was one of his favorite pastimes. He'd been in jail, he used to tell colleagues. Then, after evoking wide-eyed surprise, he'd explain that it had been because he had been a conscientious objector during World War II. But, inconsistently, he'd also claim on occasion that he'd been a Nazi hunter in his youth and explain—somewhat anticlimactically—that before the war, his father had sent him on a bicycle trip to Europe which was in fact a secret mission to kill Germans. Flamboyance was his stock in trade, self-dramatization his principal currency.

Part of his fondness for calling attention to himself took the form of mocking or painfully taunting others. When NYU, under pressure from the women's movement, printed departmental memo forms that called for the signature of a "chairperson" rather than a "chairman," Buettner-Janusch bought a stamp and inked onto each of his memos: "Please change this form! Stop defiling the English language with the vulgar neologism which I have corrected above." When he wanted to indicate to a particular professor that he had no respect for his work, he walked into the man's office and, insultingly, removed his typewriter. He was explosive with his staff during faculty meetings, and he frequently assailed his teachers' academic credentials, calling them into question, not just in front of other teachers, but even in front of students. "He actually *hounded* me from the department," said one professor, who left NYU and went to the University of Maryland. "He not only humiliated me in the presence of students but excluded me from departmental meetings." Two other professors at NYU said that after they had had certain policy differences with him, the chairman tried to curtail their responsibilities and to prevent them from having any voice in departmental decisions. He was, said a vice president of Duke University, "a fine scientist but an iconoclast of the first order, who made a lot of people mad by his statements and ultimata."

Certainly, he did make a lot of people angry. Perhaps that was why rumors of scandal trailed him wherever he went. Some colleagues said he'd plagiarized a fellow student's work when he was at the University of Michigan. (The university refused to discuss the matter.) Others said he'd mishandled the food and shelter money of an anthropological expedition he'd led while at the University of Chicago. (The charge was never pursued.) Still others said he'd never really done serious research, that the studies for which he'd become famous at Duke had actually been performed by his wife, an accomplished scientist herself.

Yet despite the rumors and his own abrasiveness, Buettner-Janusch led a charmed life in academic circles, every year garnering more and more fame and more and more research grants. But in 1977 his luck changed. That year, the National Science Foundation ceased funding him. He claimed the rejection was personal, not intellectual. Someone at NSF had it in for him, he said. But Dr. Nancie Gonzalez, an NSF program director for anthropology at the time, said, "NSF turns people down for one reason and one reason only—their work lacks scientific merit. And before such a decision is made, their proposals and their lab work are always meticulously scrutinized." Buettner-Janusch's laboratory had been visited by an NSF team; his proposals had been studied, and he had been abandoned.

It must have been a terrible shock and a serious blow to his ego, not to mention a serious incursion on his ability to do research. Without funding, he would not be able to purchase supplies, hire assistants. But that November he came up with a solution. He formed a corporation with the mocking name of Simian Expansions. Its purpose, he would eventually explain, was to raise private moneys for research on lemurs. From then on, despite his loss of federal funding, Buettner-Janusch's lab at NYU remained active, well equipped, and well populated by ambitious students.

Several graduate students signed Simian Expansions' incorporation papers, and it was they whom Richard Macris began seeing in the lab at odd hours.

By May 22, 1979, B-J knew for certain that he was under suspicion of having made illegal drugs and possibly of having planned to sell them, for he was subpoenaed to appear before a grand jury. But he seems to have believed that even if he were to be indicted, he would have no trouble clearing his name. "My lawyers have told me they can beat any charges on my reputation alone," he assured Richard Macris. And to Danny Cornyetz he confided, "The former dean of NYU law school" would soon smooth everything out by talking "like a Dutch uncle to Sawhill."

But what the chairman didn't know was that by then his students were taping him. Cooperating with the government agents—some because they feared that if they didn't, they themselves might risk the government's wrath, others because they felt morally indignant—they had agreed to spy on him, and between late May and early July they collected a number of highly incriminating statements, among them that they themselves should "deny, deny, deny" and "get busy forgetting."

Then, in August, the Drug Enforcement Agency returned to NYU and this time entered and searched a basement storeroom of the professor's, where they located a large cache of illegal drugs. (This find, however, as a result of strict privacy laws then in effect, could not be used in court.) In October 1979, Buettner-Janusch was indicted and charged with manufacturing and distributing various controlled substances as well as of conspiring to obstruct the government's investigation into the making of drugs on NYU's campus.

In July 1980, I attended his trial in the Southern District Court of New York, a trial that drew scores of friends and enemies of the charismatic professor. They sat on opposite sides of the courtroom, trying to ignore one another. The enemies had come, as might be expected, in the hope of seeing Buettner-Janusch taken down a peg. The friends had come, however, not just to lend their support, but for another reason as well. Shortly before the trial, B-J had circulated two lengthy, photocopied letters in which he implied that he was the victim of a government assault on academic freedom. In the letters, he referred to his prosecutor, a woman, as a "Nazi whore" and to the search of his storeroom as an "atrocity" resembling *Kristallnacht*, the night on which Hitler's storm-troopers smashed the property of Germany's Jews. The letters had persuaded his friends that the drug charges were senseless and that the reason he was being hounded was that the government was on a witchhunt. The issue here, his friends felt, was a scholar's right to privacy.

During breaks in the proceedings, they button-holed me, saying, "The whole thing's preposterous! A man like B-J making drugs! Why would he? He didn't need money. He's independently wealthy. And he'd have known that if he did the things the prosecution is accusing him of, he'd be risking one of the most distinguished careers in America."

Those who disliked the man were equally assertive. B-J was a sociopath, they insisted, a man without a conscience.

The evidence against Buettner-Janusch was presented by frail, hundred-pound Roanne Mann, five years out of Stanford Law, her dresses frilly and her voice little more than a loud whisper. Buettner-Janusch, she contended in her opening remarks, "used and abused his position in the academic community and turned a college lab into a drug factory." The defense counsel was Jules Rithholz, a fifty-five-year-old veteran criminal lawyer who dressed in pinstripes and delivered his questions and assertions in loud, dramatic style. "We don't deny he made drugs," Rithholz said at the start. "Of course he made drugs. But there is nothing sinister about making drugs in a laboratory." He then proceeded to explain that Buettner-Janusch's drugs had been made for legitimate research purposes. The professor had been planning to give the drugs to lemurs in order to ascertain whether neurochemicals could alter typical primate behavior. Such research was of great potential value to mankind, Rithholz argued. Why, if behavior is part chemistry and not merely a learned set of traits, "we could cure wrongdoing, we could take care of people who are recidivists, repeated criminals, and make them kindly. In one shot, we could wipe out crime."

The jury listened with interest. A majority of them had been to college. Then the prosecutor brought on the student gumshoes.

They were, in their way, hilarious—an often inept, bumbling bunch. Macris, for example, had attempted to tape not just B-J, but lab director Cornyetz as well, to see what he knew of what was going on. But he'd asked Cornyetz his probing questions while the two of them were walking in Washington Square Park, and the lab director—who'd written an anthropological treatise on punk rockers—spotted, just as they started to talk, a punky princess with glorious two-toned hair, and from then on he couldn't keep his mind on the matter under discussion. The tape revealed nothing of significance. Another tape, made by a student named Lisa Foreman, bombed out entirely. She'd worked in the lab in 1978 and noticed some of her peers "making substances" and "B-J checking on the substances." She too had decided, apparently on her own, to tape-record a conversation with Cornyetz. But she'd muffed her mission because she'd inserted not a new cassette but an old one on which she'd previously recorded herself trying to teach her parakeets to speak. "Hello. Hello. Hello. Hello," the tape had gone on endlessly in between the lab director's words. The resulting cacophany had embarrassed her, and she'd erased the recording.

But several people had made successful tapes, particularly of conversations with B-J, conversations that strongly suggested that whatever else he had been doing, he had certainly been trying to cover up a conspiracy. Macris had one on which Buettner-Janusch's voice could clearly be heard saying, "Danny has been willing to state that he was, um, the one who was messing around" and "You know what we are doing. You know what the story is, and so on. I speak in metaphors. I hope you understand what the metaphor is. And you simply stick to it." And Danny Cornyetz himself had one in which, after he reminded B-J of a discussion they had once had about making drugs, the professor responded sternly, "Danny, we're going to deny that conversation! We're going to say we were talking about something else."

On one tape, Cornyetz could be heard asking B-J, "Why did we get involved in this in the first place? . . . Is it Bruce's fault?" Bruce Greenfield was one of the students named in the incorporation papers for Simian Expansions. B-J answered, "Yes, yes it is." Cornyetz went on, "Why the——did he ever talk you into doing this?" B-J said, "Why the——am I so stupid?" And then he answered his own question: "The problem is, the point is, there is a legitimate research project buried in all of this, too."

On another Cornyetz tape, B-J could be heard declaring, "The only way they can indict one against the other is to have the others testify, and none of us have agreed to. We're too far committed."

And Professor Jolly had a tape in which B-J remarked that he wasn't worried about the charges because of his powerful friends. "I've even got the dean of the medical school at Harvard," he boasted.

When the tapes were played in the courtroom, even the chairman's friends grew suddenly silent and subdued.

I felt a fleeting flash of sympathy for the professor, particularly when listening to him ask Richard Macris, who was at the time taping him from his home in Flushing, to meet him at the lab as soon as possible. Macris said he couldn't possibly get there before one o'clock. "I have to get dressed," he announced. And then he laughed. "Dressed. And everything." From his uneasy giggle, I thought that Macris was remembering just then that in order to get ready, he had to don the body tape recorder with which the DEA agents had fitted him out. But B-J seems to have thought he meant that he had to take a shower, for he replied, "Well, then, go take a shower and get dressed and come." Macris then admitted he'd already showered, and B-J, with a sigh of perplexity, said, "Well, ah, do whatever it is you have to do to get dressed."

It is difficult not to feel sympathy toward someone

who doesn't realize he is being taped. But whatever sympathy I felt vanished when I heard B-J say, on another tape, "My law firm has got to the head U.S. Attorney and pointed out the enormous eminence I hold in the field." It is difficult to feel sympathy for someone who believes himself to be above the law.

Subsequently, B-J's predicament worsened. Danny Cornyetz testified that the chairman had said to him, "You are as amoral as the rest of us, and therefore I can tell you that we are going to make Quaaludes in the laboratory." And the Anthropology Department's administrative assistant, a graduate student named Richard Dorfman, testified that not only had B-J told him, too, that drugs would be made in the lab but that eventually he gave him some lab-produced synthetic cocaine and asked him to sell it.

He did so, Dorfman said. It was just a tiny bit of cocaine, a mere $100 worth. He kept $20 for himself and handed over the remaining $80 to B-J.

The defense attorney's cast of characters was, of course, different. To prove the point that the anthropologist had made drugs in his lab only because he had intended to use them on lemurs, Rithholz produced a Chicago fund-raiser named Pat Pronger, who had been employed to raise money for Simian Expansions. Among the specific budgetary requests that Buettner-Janusch had made of her was money with which to purchase lemurs, for, as he'd explained to her, he intended to do a behavior-modification study on these animals. But Pronger's testimony misfired, for it became clear as she was cross-examined that the professor had requested only enough funds for two or three lemurs, or two or three females and their "husbands," as she put it. These few animals would not have been sufficient to justify the large amounts of drugs that had been found.

Rithholz also put on the stand a group of character witnesses who testified that they considered Buettner-Janusch honest and trustworthy. But their testimony, too, seemed inadequate since, as the prosecutor pointed out, they'd known B-J in past, not recent, days. Finally, Rithholz suggested—confusingly—that perhaps Buettner-Janusch hadn't, after all, been making drugs. Perhaps Christopher Jolly, jealous of B-J and covetous of his position, had planted them in the lab.

The suggestion went nowhere. Jolly, with his longish hair and wry smile, looked disarmingly like an engaging, early Beatle, and no matter how hard Rithholz pressed him, he refused to admit to harboring any ill feelings toward the chairman. He did admit he'd been a scavenger, searching through garbage pails, and that he'd been sneaky, never confronting B-J with his suspicions. But he said that B-J's imperiousness required that he act surreptitiously. And he convincingly conveyed the impression that he'd been motivated soley by honor, by an old-fashioned view of the responsibilities of his profession, and by outrage over what he suspected was happening in the lab.

Buettner-Janusch didn't take the stand, and at last, after ten days of testimony, the prosecution and the defense summed up.

The jury deliberated for less than five hours and found Buettner-Janusch guilty on two counts involving the manufacture with intent to sell of LSD, methaqualone, and synthetic cocaine and two counts of lying to federal investigators. The one count on which he was found not guilty concerned the distribution of the drug cylert pemoline, a stimulant. No, he hadn't done *that*, the jury said.

That afternoon, as I left the courthouse, I felt I understood B-J's motivation for becoming involved in making drugs. It hadn't been just to make money. There exist in society certain individuals who believe themselves to be endowed with such extravagant, even imperial, intelligence that they feel it their destiny to conquer worlds, command obeisance, cancel the rules by which ordinary mortals live. To such people, safety seems boring, banal. And outwitting society becomes, in a way, a hobby. Buettner-Janusch, who detested banality and prided himself on his wits, had wanted to pit his brains against the system.

But why had his students gone along with him? I found that quite puzzling, and, in search of an answer, I went that afternoon to the NYU campus. Summer session was in progress, and the park that borders the school was filled with students energetically taking notes on the grass, the corridors bustling with bright and eager young faces.

I took an elevator to the office of the Anthropology Department, hoping I might find some of the students who'd worked in B-J's lab. During the trial, they had been enjoined from talking to reporters, but perhaps now they would open up.

I was fortunate, indeed. There was Richard Dorfman, the administrative assistant who'd sold the synthetic cocaine for B-J. He'd said at the trial that he'd done it in order to keep his job. But I wanted to know why he'd participated in the first stages of the scheme, the creation of the drugs. Hadn't he felt any concern about that, any sense that it was wrong or at least that he might, if he participated, be putting his career at risk?

Dorfman listened to my questions and began to speak. "You come to a lab where drugs are being made, and you feel imprisoned, but after a while, your sense of reality becomes distorted and you accept what's going on. You go along with what's happening. Sometimes the path of least resistance is the easiest path."

Later, I mentioned Dorfman's comments to a professor in the Anthropology Department and she nodded thoughtfully. "You get the feeling, when you talk with the kids who were involved, that they felt the kind of sneaky, pervasive fear that people always develop in the face of true psychosis," she said. "It's not the shaking-in-the-boots kind of terror. But it's terror just the same. And it makes people want to just look the other way, to want not to ask themselves too many questions. You know, B-J was always talking about Hitler, and how the government was using Hitlerian tactics on him. But, in fact, the way the students feared his power, and went along with him, makes you understand the rise of Hitler."

Buettner-Janusch was sentenced to jail for five years. Clifford Jolly continued to teach at NYU. Richard Dorfman got fired. Richard Macris gave up anthropology for business administration. And Danny Cornyetz gave up anthropology to make tapes for a company that supplied museums with recorded art lectures.

About the Author

Linda Wolfe is the author of two previous works of nonfiction, PLAYING AROUND and THE LITERARY GOURMET, and of PRIVATE PRACTICES, a novel. She has written for a variety of magazines, among them *New York*, of which she is a contributing editor. She lives in New York City.